No
Yelling

The 9 Secrets of
Marine Corps Leadership
You Must Know to
Win in Business

Wally Adamchik

FireStarter Speaking and Consulting

Library of Congress Cataloging in Publication

ISBN: 0-9779005-0-9

Originally published by James & Brookfield Publishers

ISBN: 0-9771912-0-6

Printed in the United States of America

10 9 8 7 6 5 4 3 2

To My Family
Pam, Mogie, and BJ
Dad, Mom, and Billy
And the many others

To All Marines
Past
Present
Future

A portion of the proceeds from this book will be
donated to help injured Marines and their families.

Table of Contents

Introduction

Japan, January, 1987—You are at my side in an M-60 tank. We are conducting a tactical training exercise at the base of Mount Fuji, operating as part of a Marine battalion, working jointly with the Japanese Ground Self-Defense Force. Two days into the exercise, snow begins falling heavily. Of course, battles don't stop because of bad weather and neither does training. But the snow continues, and our tanks do not have winter cleats on their tracks. We're in a sixty-ton vehicle on the side of a mountain, sliding on ice, with no control. With the situation now unsafe, the battalion calls "time-out," and we occupy defensive positions as part of the now-changed scenario.

We gather our four other tank commanders and explain the situation. We acknowledge the uncertainty, but remind the men that there is work to be done. I leave them with this statement as they go back to their tanks and their own crews: *"I'll be in my tank. Call me with questions. Just make sure you are doing something productive."*

An hour or so later, the Company Executive Officer is knocking on our tank and he is very agitated. *"The CO (commanding officer) wants to see you. Now! He's over on the main road in his jeep."* We trudge through the snow several hundred yards to see the Captain. He is red with rage.

"Adamchik, what do you think you are doing?"

"Sir?"

*"The battalion commander and I are touring the area and everything is fine—until we come to your platoon. I told him I would take care of it. Now, what the *&$% is that?"* he demands, pointing to one of our vehicles.

In front of the tank are two snowmen. More precisely, a snow-man and a snowwoman. We know they are man and woman because they are anatomically correct. I am speechless.

"Well, what is that?"

"Ummm, it looks like a snowman and—woman, Sir. Actually it is a snowcouple."

"Really... and **why** *are they there during our tactical exercise? Did they teach you this at Ft. Knox as some new security measure? Or are you just trying to embarrass me in front of the Battalion Commander?"*

"No, Sir. I told the men to do something productive. I was not as explicit as I should have been."

"No, you weren't! Now, go fix this! Is that explicit enough for you?" And he is gone in his jeep.

What a lesson in communication! I have never forgotten it. I told our people to do something productive, and they did. They didn't go to sleep. They didn't wander around. They built snow-people—a snow couple. What else might a couple of nineteen-year-olds do in a snowstorm? Yet, in this (now) comical moment is a powerful example of the importance of clear communication in leadership. In the coming pages, we will look at actual examples and lessons on various aspects of leading people.

You might ask, *"Why should these stories matter to me?"* Your inbox is probably full. And it's likely to stay that way. You're already busy, and the challenges of the marketplace and life are not getting any easier. Is it even possible to work harder? How many more late nights, weekends, and overtime can you—or your people—stand? The reason these examples are important is that you can learn from them. And through applying the learning comes relief, relief from the late nights, overtime, and frustration, and relief in the form of an engaged and energized workforce.

Bosses lament and surveys show that too many workers are watching the clock, biding their time until they can go home. They show up day after day, uninspired, giving far less than one hundred percent of themselves to the job. Companies following this "work as drudgery" model are marked for extinction.

The organizations that thrive in the coming decades will be the ones that *energize* their employees. Machines and technology will only take you so far. The difference between success and failure is in the *people* in the organization—the very ones you are leading. The knowledge and information economy of the new millennium presents new challenges. Yet, effective leadership remains the key that unlocks the drive and desire in employees so that they, and the organization, win. And when that happens, you win. Effective leadership can be learned.

US Marines are known and respected the world over for their leadership ability. How do they do it? What do they know that enables them to be such successful leaders on active duty and then in the civilian sector? While other books talk about having a strategy, NO YELLING shows you how to *execute* the strategy and *accomplish the mission* with your people. Using information from more than 100 interviews, we now reveal to you the principles of leadership that are the hallmark of the United States Marines. Not the ones from a textbook but the on-the-job, proven successful principles. Most importantly, you will learn that these principles are easily applied with success in the civilian sector.

Other books that advocate the use of military leadership in the business world share two basic weaknesses.

- First, they are often written at the strategic level, purely from an executive perspective. Therefore, they are not applicable to the majority of leaders and managers in business. Most people in business don't sit at the executive level of a very large enterprise. Of the nation's five million employers, 75 percent employ fewer than 10 workers. Very few of those that do work in Fortune 500 companies are in executive positions. The truth is that the majority of people are leading on a smaller and more personal scale that is largely neglected in much of the literature on leadership.

- Second, many of these books *tell* you what to do, but they do not back up their directives with real-life examples that enable you to see how to do it. This book makes clear the effects of well- and poorly executed leadership on the outcome of actual business and military situations. The anecdotes come from active-duty Marines and from former Marines, all successful, now working in the civilian sector. The intent is for you to draw clear parallels with your specific situation to illustrate that *what works on active duty works in business.*

Leadership is a conscious behavior, developed through application and ongoing assessment. It is both an art, learned and refined over time, and a skill that requires practice and introspection. It's what makes people **want** to work for you. And, as you will see, it's about trust. Successful leaders *earn* the trust of those they lead, allowing them to advance their agenda in support of the larger effort.

Each chapter features a thorough discussion of a particular leadership principle, complete with business and military examples. You will find end-of-chapter questions and suggestions for study. These enable you to think as a leader, whether you're relaxing at home in the recliner, or honing your employees' skills in the training room. Another excellent use for this section is group study and discussion as part of ongoing leadership development. You may wish to target one leadership area each month to maintain a concerted focus on leader development.

For additional support in this effort, I encourage you to sign up for monthly email reinforcements that will help you keep the topic top-of-mind. Visit the website at *www.noyelling.net* to register. These reminders will help you retain the key principles and apply them. This is an important step because you become a better leader only through the conscious application of these points.

As you read specific examples of these leadership principles, you'll naturally begin to compare them with your own experiences. You will also think of ways you can implement the ideas in your environment. When this happens, I encourage you to *write your thoughts in the margins*. Simply thinking about what you've read is not enough. *Action is required!* Your notes serve as the foundation for your action-planning and enable you to implement these principles successfully.

My path as a leader is filled with lows (snowmen) and highs (pinning 2nd Lieutenant bars on the shoulders of someone I influenced—the nineteen-year-old who built the snowman several years earlier). Your path will be similar. But at the end of the day, when you can look in the mirror and know you did the right thing, or when you receive an unexpected letter from someone you influenced "way back when," you'll be glad you ventured down the path. There are others who need your leadership. So continue down the path—all the while, making a positive impact on people and our society. Not bad for a day's work.

Semper Fidelis,

Wally Adamchik

Integrity

Trustworthy
Consistent
Non-negotiables

Integrity is what you do when it doesn't matter, when no one will ever know what you did. Integrity is more than what you do; it is who you are.
John Russell III,
Captain USMC
President
Russell Construction Services

In these perilous times which face mankind and the world over, I would like to stress the moral and ethical side of leadership responsibility. For it is in the area of moral courage, truth, and honor that the fibers of character are strengthened sufficiently to sustain men under the great stresses and responsibility facing our military leaders today.
General David M. Shoup USMC
World War II

In the post-Enron world of the early-21st century, *integrity*, and its cousin *ethics*, are words that get plenty of air time and even more lip-service. They're tossed around carelessly, but the deeper, more difficult, dialogue on *what integrity is* and *why it matters* is critically absent.

Your own definition of integrity may involve nuances different from the CEO across town. Ultimately, however, the quality of integrity is based on strong values. It is the most-cited response to survey questions of what employees want in a boss. This top-ranking transcends generations and cultures. Universally, people want to work for someone they can trust.

Steelcase, the office equipment manufacturer, regularly conducts surveys of the worldwide office environment. In 1991, being honest, upright, and ethical were very important to 87 percent of Canadians and 72 percent of Japanese respondents. Jim Kouzes and Larry Posner, in *Leadership is a Relationship*, cite honesty as *the most important supervisory trait* in every study they have done since 1981. Over the years, no fewer than 87 percent of respondents listed honesty as number one.

TRUSTWORTHY

In the chapter "Commander's Intent," we will look at the implied trust from leader to follower. Integrity is the corollary to commander's intent. It is the trait that sends the message, "You can trust me to guide you in the right direction and to watch out for you."

The reciprocal of trust is leadership in its most basic form. A leader says, "Here is what I want you to do, and I trust you to do it." The follower says, "I will do it because I trust you to do the right thing."

Those unfamiliar with the military will cite the captive employee aspect that mandates compliance by a subordinate. And yes, unfortunately there are examples of people in leadership positions in the military—and in the civilian sector—who rely on the power of their position to get the job done. These so-called "leaders" are opportunistic and self-serving, and not true leaders at all. Ultimately, the assigned task does get done, but usually less effectively in a situation in which the leader relies on positional power.

The more-enlightened leader uses influence to accomplish the objective and acts with integrity. It is only the weak military leader who resorts to, "I am ordering you to do this." Such comments are more often seen on television than in real life. The captive employee knows the rules and will comply with them. He respects the *position* occupied by the weak leader but *not the leader.*

Power comes from several sources. In this case, we are looking at positional power and influence power. **Positional power** is based on the box someone occupies on the organizational chart. **Influence power** comes from one's credibility and integrity. It can be exercised at *any* level of the organizational chart. Think of the old-timer who has been around for years, working in the ranks. Everyone looks up to him because of his *experience and character*, not his *title*.

Truly effective leaders don't rely on positional power. They are masters of influence. They do a great job, in the words of Ken Maney, Lt Col USMC, *of getting people to want to do something that they might not necessarily have wanted to do on their own.* This concept of leadership was offered by many interviewed for this book.

In initial Marine officer training at The Basic School in Quantico, Virginia, the concept of integrity is so deeply instilled in young lieutenants that their response, even years later, is almost automatic. When asked, "What is the most important leadership trait?" *integrity* is the universal response. How, then, do leaders manifest it, and how do they measure it in others? Through truth, honesty, consistency, and respect—in public and private.

According to Rob Peterman, Major USMC, *"Leaders gain credibility through the truth. They don't get it by exaggerating and they don't get it by sugar-coating. The truth, good or bad, is the key element in building credibility. The people we lead are not stupid. They know some of the truth and they know when a leader doesn't tell them the rest of the story. If that happens, that leader is done."*

The leader with integrity does not use the Chicken Little school of motivation—that is, by declaring an emergency of "The sky is falling!" proportions. Nor do leaders cry wolf by generating a false deadline and a false sense of urgency. The leader with integrity assigns deadlines based on the needs and realities of the task at hand, and explains why the task matters and why it must be accomplished by a given time.

Marine Example

We were in the final stages of getting ready for a two-week field exercise in advance of a six-month deployment to the Mediterranean. The Battalion Commander was going to conduct a final inspection on Friday at 11 AM, before we went on a long weekend. When we returned on Tuesday at noon, we would move to the field.

Shortly after this plan was announced, my Company Commander informed us that *he* would conduct an inspection at 8 AM on Friday, and he strongly suggested that we Platoon Commanders do an inspection the day prior, to make sure all was ready, and then *re-inspect* early on Friday to make sure all was ready for his inspection. These inspections involved displaying all the gear and equipment we would bring with us to the field, as well as the vehicles we would use. They were time-consuming and quite detailed.

Essentially, the Marines would have to lay everything out and pack it all up several times to be ready for the Battalion Commander's inspection. I offered to my men that I thought we could be more efficient and asked what they thought. They all agreed that *one* pre-inspection by the tank commanders would be enough. They formulated a plan that would allow them to have everything in place on Friday by 7 AM. I asked if they really thought they could get it done right; they assured me they could. So, I told them to go ahead with their plan.

While the other platoons showed up on Friday at 4 AM, we didn't show up until 6:30 AM. At 7 AM, my guys were as ready as the guys who had been preparing for days. Neither the Battalion Commander nor his staff could find anything wrong with my platoon. The other two platoons each had a few discrepancies—even after earlier pre-inspections.

Now, the overall performance of the Company in the inspection wasn't bad, but the CO wanted *perfection*, so he made us all come to work at 6 AM the following Tuesday although originally we were supposed to come to work at noon. Yet, in taking more and more free time away from the Marines by adding unnecessary inspections, he was saying, in effect, "I don't trust you to prepare correctly." Further, he was taking them away from their families when, soon, they would be taken away from them for six months. This lack of trust and unfair treatment basically *guaranteed* things to go wrong. Yet, my guys never let me down. They said, "Trust us." I did, and everything worked out perfectly.

Jeff Schade
Captain USMC
Consultant
National consulting firm

The leader with integrity delivers *personal feedback*. Rather than always telling the group some generic or hollow comment, he specifically points out what the group or an individual did. He doesn't say, "Nice job today." He says, "Jim, nice job on the accuracy of the numbers on that report."

This is important because: 1) Jim knows it's true and appreciates the recognition, or 2) Jim doesn't know it's true and needs the positive reinforcement to continue the behavior. But what Jim and his co-workers know for sure is that a generic comment can be applied to anyone for any situation. It makes no personal impact. Good leaders also deliver candid feedback—what I call "brutal honesty." They're not afraid to tell it like it is.

When I am working for someone who has integrity, at least I know where I stand. If I am in good standing, great. I want to keep doing the things I'm doing to stay there. If I am in bad standing, at least I now know it, and I'm able to make changes to what I'm doing.

Roger Brown
Captain USMC
Project manager
National technology firm

In fact, those we lead expect to be held accountable. The leader who overlooks problems sends the message that the standards are variable.

Marine Example

It is not all about being a nice guy. When I make my rounds I tell them when things are not right. But I make the situation an instructional one. I may ask a question about why something is not operating correctly, and that leads into a discussion of how to get it fixed or why it's important to get it operating correctly. Our people really do want to do good work. We just need to give them the guidance and encouragement, sometimes in the form of corrective action, to get it done.

People expect to be held accountable. We grew up with the concept. Parents, teachers, coaches all held us accountable. As adults, we want it, too, but we don't want to be treated like children. Of course, for me to hold my people accountable, I must hold myself accountable. Ultimately, excellence is a shared commitment. We know the standards and we work together to achieve them.

Jim Chartier
Lt Col USMC

CONSISTENT

People with integrity deliver on the commitments they make and accept by knowing not only their own capability and workload, but also those of their team. They don't over-commit. They are able to say no and explain why. When they do say yes, they get the job done. If they later find that they cannot get it done, they quickly get help and notify the appropriate people.

Civilian Example

The company president described himself as a nice guy who wanted people to perform well. His parent company implemented a new procedure that necessitated new reports. The president needed information from his direct reports, the regional managers, to accurately submit his report. He told them he wanted the information by February 7. The day came and passed with no information from the regional managers.

I visited with him on February 23 and he complained about his regional managers. He related that they never gave him the information he wanted on time. I asked if he had talked with them on the days immediately after February 7, and, of course, the answer was no. This was standard practice at this company. He squandered his credibility with his managers because of his failure to hold them accountable. His integrity was suspect, not in the sense that he was a liar, but in the sense that he did not live up to his word or his directives. His behavior then encouraged people to not deliver on commitments and requests because no one was looking for them to do it. Even worse, there were no negative repercussions for failure to perform.

Wally Adamchik
Major USMCR
Consultant

Civilian Example

I took over a group of people that was not per-forming at the level they needed to, or that they were capable of. We have a requirement to conduct monthly one-on-one meetings with our team members. The prior manager didn't do them. He viewed them as a waste of time since they didn't result in production.

When I took over, I set up a meeting schedule for the next three months. I also set a standard agenda, so everyone on my team would know how to prepare for these meetings.

I made it a top priority to conduct the meetings as scheduled. In the first three months, I never post-poned or rescheduled one. And over the course of the year, we conducted 96 percent of them as scheduled.

Very quickly, the group learned that I am consis-tent in my actions and that I deliver on my commit-ments. Most important, they know they matter to me. This process gave me credibility with them; we did a lot of great work after that.

Roger Brown
Captain UMSC
Project manager
National technology firm

The leader with integrity adheres to one standard. A concept instilled in all Marine leaders is that of eating last. The leader of a unit will not sit down to a meal until each of his Marines has gotten food. Not only is he taking care of his Marines by making sure they are fed, but he is sending the message that *one standard applies to all.* Senior Marines don't retreat to some mess tent away from the troops where the food is better and the air is cleaner. There is no executive washroom in the Marines.

Leaders with integrity can take bad news, especially when it is aimed at them. They don't shoot the messenger; they acknowledge when they are wrong. This honesty makes them approachable. Leaders who are approachable know what is going on in their units.

People with integrity aren't defensive. They know when they are right and they will defend their position. But they do so with grace and an even temper. They also know when they are wrong and will accept correction.

Marine Example

I was present while the battery conducted live fire exercises. The most egregious sin in artillery is misdirecting a round (artillery shell) to land outside the target impact area. This is called "firing out." Not only is it inaccurate, but it is incredibly dangerous as the round may land in a populated area, causing death or destruction. On this particular day, the unit fired out.

Several officers, who were not in the operational chain of command, witnessed the incident and were called before the Battalion Commander. Several of these were truly innocent bystanders, but now their careers were on the line. As we stood at attention, he asked us very pointed questions about how such an occurrence was allowed to happen. It was not unusual in this kind of circumstance for all the officers involved to be relieved of duty—a major black mark on their record and a potentially career-ending event. Having gathered the facts, the Battalion Commander continued protocol, saying, "Let's go see the Regimental Commander."

The scene was repeated, except this time, the Battalion Commander stood at attention, too. When asked what had happened and why, he explained that the misjudgment of an inexperienced section chief resulted in the firing out. He added, for clarification, that there was nothing the officers in the room could have done to change what had happened. But the Battalion Commander's integrity shone strongest in his next statement.

He told the regimental commander, *"Sir, these are my men and this was my unit. The section chief was in that position because my staff assigned him there. You can look to no one but me for this error."* The Regimental Commander agreed and dismissed the officers. The case was closed and dropped. The Regimental Commander told me later that, had the Battalion Commander tried to avoid responsibility or offer some excuse, he would have relieved us all. He thought there was more learning for us in seeing the loyalty and professionalism of our boss rewarded.

Word of the Battalion Commander's actions traveled quickly through the ranks. His loyalty to his men, and his willingness to take the hit for us, earned him even greater loyalty from them. We all knew he could have easily pointed the finger at his junior officers. The fact that he chose to shoulder the responsibility himself elevated his status, and his effectiveness, as a leader.

Rod Long
Lt Col USMCR
Account executive
Technology company

A leader with integrity will take the time to talk about integrity with his people. Many of Enron's leaders, for example, had integrity, initially. But they allowed themselves to slide down the slippery slope. Had they taken time, periodically, to talk about integrity in decision-making, the outcome for that entire corporation might have been different.

Acting with integrity lets your employees know what to expect because integrity is based on values, and values are constant. The leader who is mercurial in his behavior creates workers who behave less like confident members of the organization and more like dogs who were beaten as puppies. Of course, we don't physically harm our people, but if we berate them verbally, in no time at all, they'll be cowering whenever we approach.

Credibility based on integrity is developed and reinforced one interaction at a time. The majority of people will give you the benefit of the doubt initially. They generally assume you have integrity. Your actions, particularly those behind closed doors, will confirm or deny that assumption.

Marine Example

A squadron commander is the ultimate decision-maker for his unit. He is charged with setting the tone for the squadron through the use of commander's intent and proper conduct. However, one commander didn't think this was necessary.

Publicly, he said and did all the right things. He looked good in uniform, was proficient at his job, and treated subordinates with respect.

Behind closed doors, he revealed his true self. In meetings, he would talk poorly about absent squadron members. He criticized his boss to others, although never directly to the boss. And he liberally (and creatively) interpreted the standards when reporting information about his squadron to make himself look good to his superiors.

Although he performed his job well enough, he avoided flying dangerous night missions. This behavior diminished his credibility with his own pilots. Further, he reduced night training for the entire squadron to the bare minimum, in the ill-considered notion that the less the unit flew at night, the less chance there would be for a mishap that would mar his record.

During a particularly difficult night training mission, one of the aircraft crashed. (Fortunately, no one was injured.) The ensuing investigation determined a primary reason for the mishap to be the lack of adequate training prior to the flight. The commander's self-centered desire to mitigate risk actually *increased* risk, endangering his Marines and his equipment. (Such a minimal amount of night training would have been disastrous in combat.)

His behavior was neither illegal nor cause for removal from command. But if you surveyed his Marines, he would have been "voted off the island." They disliked and distrusted him, which led them to perform at the bare minimum. He was someone they avoided in the halls and derided after work. Morale plummeted.

The long-term impact of this individual's "leadership" is still felt today, more than a decade later. Re-enlistment rates for Marines from that unit were lower than for similar units. Good Marines who could have made an ongoing and positive impact on the Corps chose to quit after their experience under his command. In trying to look out for himself instead of his men, he damaged the organization—in the destruction of a multi-million dollar aircraft, but more importantly in lower retention of key people.

Compare that example to this more favorable one:

Marine Example

Another Squadron Commander, in a similar situation to that of the aforementioned Commander, chose to work differently with his

Marines. He flew in all the difficult missions and actively participated in the debriefing—as a member of the flight, *not* as the commander. In these debriefings, he candidly discussed his actions during the mission, and, if he made a mistake, pointed the finger at himself. His candor greatly enhanced the quality of the debriefing. From such leadership, the pilots learned not only how to do a better job next time, but how to model integrity and character.

Not surprisingly, outsiders recognized this squadron for its high level of performance. Internally, the morale was extremely high. Decades later, squadron members recount that period as the best time of their career.

NON-NEGOTIABLES

Too frequently, people look at the world in black and white. And that black and white is based on their values, skills, ability, and experience. An activity or decision being evaluated is labeled either right or wrong—depending on the perspective of the one doing the evaluating. But the reality is that leaders need to be comfortable with a wide gray area that allows individual action and flexibility for the subordinate.

When I coach leaders, one of the first exercises I ask them to work through is their "non-negotiables" list. This process gets to one of the classic leadership conversations: Do you want those following you to follow a *specified path* to achieve the desired result, or do you want the *desired result*?

The answer to both questions is, "Yes." *Sometimes* you will want them to follow a specific path; this is a non-negotiable. More often, you are interested in the result and, as long as your people act with integrity during the process (they didn't break any rules, didn't hurt anyone), then it doesn't matter how they got there. This is the gray area that leaders need to get comfortable with.

Often, the technical competence of the leader is a major barrier here. The leader has a preferred way of performing a given task. As a supervisor, he may be quick to correct an employee doing the task differently. He is evaluating the *method* rather than the *result*. He is also exercising *control* instead of *influence*. But controlling is not leading.

There are compelling reasons to let the employee continue without intervening. First and foremost, she might find a better way to accomplish the assigned task. Second, she might discover on her own that the supervisor's method really was better. Third, it might not matter how the assignment is done, as long as the desired result is reached.

Integrity matters here because the non-negotiables need to be communicated to employees (commander's intent). Then, they must be maintained and upheld. Over time, a valid reason may arise to change a non-negotiable. A new technology allows a new procedure that previously would have been unsafe, for example. In the absence of any mitigating circumstances, non-negotiables are just that: not open for debate. They are the things that must *always* be done. Violation of a non-negotiable must *always* generate a conversation with the leader. It may result in some type of disciplinary action. It will not be swept under the rug. It will not be ignored. If it is explained away or easily dismissed, then it is not truly a non-negotiable. And if this happens, all the other so-called non-negotiables the leader had previously communicated become optional. The leader has lost credibility.

Some of your non-negotiables may be procedures outlined in your operations manual (however, *not all* of your operational procedures are non-negotiable). If a procedure is in your manual and you allow it to be ignored, what message are you sending? Deviation from procedures should *always* be addressed. If not, employees get the message that the procedures manual is optional. Then the results become variable and anarchy sets in. Deviation from a non-negotiable should be addressed in an intense and forthright manner.

Checklists are a highly effective tool to help ensure consistent performance. Used correctly, they contribute to profitability and employee development. Leaders who are confident and recognize the impact on the organization will use checklists. Unfortunately, two situations come to mind in which people disregard using the checklist. Senior employees who have been doing the work for years probably don't need to use a checklist and they generally don't use one. The problem here is that they are being a poor role model for new leaders. Additionally, as procedures change, in not using the checklist they will continue to use the old way. On the other end of the spectrum is the new supervisor who, out of insecurity or over-confidence, neglects to use the checklist. In each of these cases the risk is missed steps with corresponding negative results.

Every aircraft in the world has checklists for the crew to reference. There are procedures for starting, stopping and everything in-between from the routine to the emergency. Procedures require that the checklist always be used. In a two-pilot aircraft, the process is known as challenge and response: one pilot reads the action required (the challenge) in the checklist, and the other replies accordingly (the response) as he executes the task.

Despite the fact that using checklists is required, pilots sometimes skip them altogether, or run through them alone, instead of taking advantage of the additional safeguard of challenge and response with the other pilot. There are seemingly valid reasons for this. Perhaps the co-pilot is arriving late at the aircraft, so the pilot begins the procedures early to ensure an on-time takeoff. Or, maybe the pilot is so comfortable starting the aircraft, having done it hundreds of times before, that he simply thinks he doesn't need the checklist.

Marine Example

We were late for the launch and hustling to get airborne and get on station. I was the pilot. I told the co-pilot to check on a few final things and meet me at the bird. We had done the pre-flight check of the plane earlier in the morning so all we had to do was hop in and get it started. I got strapped in and waited for the co-pilot. It was hot, I was baking in the cockpit, and we were running late, so I decided to start the plane—at least, I could get the air conditioning going! As I was finishing getting the first engine online, and was getting ready to start the second, my co-pilot came aboard, strapped in, and got situated with his maps. A few minutes later, we were talking to the tower and were on our way to support our infantry unit.

A short time into the hop, all the gauges went to zero. The first thing that went through my mind was, "The engines are still working, so we're not going to fall out of the sky." I looked down to see that my batteries had gone dead. I realized my generators weren't on. I had never turned on my generators. I reached over, flipped them both on, and immediately, the gauges start working and we had power. No big deal? Sure. Routine? No. Had this been a night flight, I would have lost not only my gauges, but all of the lights, too. Then, things could have gotten really dicey. I might have had to fumble for my flashlight. I might not have discovered the problem as quickly, and that could have led to a mishap. What if we had been on a gun run? That could have proven fatal. Who knows? I do know that I started the airplane without using the checklist and that is why my generators were not on.

For me, using the checklist became a non-negotiable. If I was the pilot, I asked the co-pilot to read the challenge and response from the checklist. If I was the co-pilot, I made sure the pilot knew of my desire to use the checklist; I never had anyone tell me no.

I went to the airplane once for a training mission and the trainee, who had been around for a year or so, had started the airplane. He was in the pilot seat for this training mission. I was acting as the co-pilot as well as the instructor. He had briefed in our preflight briefing that we would use challenge and response when using the checklist from startup to shutdown. Yet, here we were and he had started the plane without me. I hopped in, strapped in, and broke out my checklist to review the start procedures to make sure he didn't miss anything—which I knew could happen. When I started to go through the checklist, he blew me off and told me it was started and he was ready to go. I acknowledged that but said we should just run through it anyway. He came back with a comment about how we would miss our range time and he would not get his certification if we missed the time we were supposed to be on the range. I told him to shut the airplane down and read through the shutdown procedures. Once we were out of the airplane, I let him vent a bit and told him I would meet him in the ready room in fifteen minutes. I checked in with operations and asked if they could squeeze me into a range time our squadron had in a few hours, and they were able to do it. I then met with the pilot and explained several things to him. First, using a checklist was a non-negotiable for me, which I had already told him. Second, he had briefed that we would use the checklist and then he chose not to. This caused me to wonder what else he might not do that he had said he was going to do. We talked openly and candidly about the situation. He was receptive and then I told him about the new range time. And we turned our attention to the new flight.

Of course, word quickly got out in the squadron and I was fine with that. As an instructor pilot I needed to set the standard. If I didn't follow the rules and if I didn't adhere to the flight brief, I would have

been sending the message that those polices and procedures really didn't matter. And then we would have
pilots doing whatever they wanted to, and that was a
recipe for a mishap.

Jon Hackett
Major USMC

Civilian Example

A national consulting firm instituted an annual
employee satisfaction survey and connected a portion
of each branch manager's compensation to the results
of that survey. Employee issues were often subordi-
nated to client demands, and the CEO of the company wanted to do better in this area. He made it a
priority. In the first year of the survey, predictably,
there was a wide variance in the scores of the
numerous locations. Two managers, both of whom
produced good financial results for the company,
scored near the bottom that year. They chose very
different courses of action to improve their scores in
the next year's survey.

Manager A immediately gathered his people and
shared the information with them. He then asked
them for more detail on what they meant and why
they had scored the branch that way. He facilitated a
discussion for several hours, and then wrote a memo
back to his staff summarizing the discussion. He then
asked his people to form and serve on committees to
address the major issues uncovered in the survey and
the discussion. The process he used was later adopted
at many other branches because other managers saw
the great improvement in his second-year scores.

Manager B initially took no action. When the survey was administered the second time, he gathered

his staff and told them that his compensation was partly based on the results of the survey and that he expected they would work with him to make sure his scores were better this year. He then distributed the survey and had everyone complete it in his presence. He thanked them for their support and promised to take care of them. One of those employees made an anonymous call to Human Resources at corporate headquarters. The complaint was investigated, and the manager was fired.

Anonymous
National consulting firm

There is another lesson here about integrity. While the integrity of Manager B was clearly questionable, the integrity of the CEO to fire this manager is noteworthy. The manager produced good financial results but behaved incorrectly. In firing this manager, the CEO reaffirmed his non-negotiable of taking care of employees. This attitude is rare. More often the sole determinant of performance is financial. It is not unusual to find bosses who exhibit any number of generally unacceptable behaviors yet who are permitted to remain in position because they produce good numbers. Senior leaders must address, and document, this poor behavior.

SUMMARY

Integrity is about tangible actions for an intangible concept and is the foundational element of leadership. People do not want to follow a leader they cannot trust. If they are forced to follow that leader, they will do the bare minimum needed to get by.

Integrity dictates the same behavior, whether in public or in private. Consistency, delivering on commitments, and maintaining standards are all facets of integrity.

A bit of advice Marines often hear before going on liberty in port applies to integrity and ethical decision-making: *would you want your mother to know what you are doing?* For you the question may be, *would you want this to be on the front page of USA Today?*

Integrity matters because it enables you to have real relationships based on trust. And when we trust each other, we can excel together. And when we excel together we are having fun together.

Mark Rullman
Captain USMC (deceased)

End of chapter application for
individual consideration and group discussion

1. Describe your own personal code of integrity.

2. What are your non-negotiables at work?

3. What are your non-negotiables in life?

4. Does your firm have an ethics policy and do people know it?

5. If not, should there be one? Why or why not?

6. Describe a situation in which you acted with integrity. Be specific. How did you feel about this situation and your behavior?

7. Describe a situation in which you witnessed someone else acting with integrity. How did that behavior make you feel about that person?

8. Describe a situation in which an individual acted without integrity or in contradiction to your ethics policy. How did that affect your opinion of that person?

9. What risks are there for you, and your firm, if you make a decision that is viewed as lacking integrity?

10. Would your mother be pleased with the decisions you are making and the way you are behaving?

Technical Competence

The Foundation of Credibility
Success Triangle
Setting the Standards

The facts are that times change, technology changes, weapons change, but basic human nature doesn't change. A leader must keep up-to-date on every aspect of his job, weigh all facts, and seek other people's advice.
General Lewis H. Wilson
Quoted in Karel Montor et al.,
Naval Leadership; Voices of Experience, 1987

As a new platoon commander, you are trained to be a squad leader on steroids, breaking trail in the snow, land navigation, going on every patrol. But I was trying too hard to prove myself. I now know I don't need to do it all.
Jimmy Lane
Captain USMC

There is a high expectation that the leader be competent in the assigned task or specialty he is supervising. This expectation exists to some level in all endeavors. Workers want the boss to know what they do and to have, at least, a rudimentary understanding of how it is done. At a minimum, the leader should be familiar with the task. Even better, he should have some proficiency at it. The Marine who might be in combat someday will want to know: "Does this guy in charge know his job, and *my* job, well enough so that he doesn't get me *killed*?"

But there is more to it than that.

Decisions are better when you are grounded and understand the systems, procedures, tools, equipment, tactics, and structure.

Stephen Oren
Col USMC retired
Business owner

The Foundation of Credibility

Not all military service members are frontline trigger-pullers. Many support the trigger-pullers as logisticians, administrators, and mechanics, to name just a few positions. These specialists consistently cite the importance of technical competence in their leaders. First, this is a respect issue. Second, it is a direction issue. Employees correctly believe that if the boss doesn't know what they do and how they do it, she will be unable to make the right decisions on how to effectively employ them, implement changes that positively impact performance, and improve the team's ability to capitalize on future opportunities. `

Even more important is the willingness of the leader to admit when she doesn't know how to do something. Those Marines (and employees) who do the task daily don't expect the leader to be an expert on the task they routinely perform. They do expect her to be familiar with it and to take an interest in it. When the supervisor asks questions about what the employees are doing and *sincerely* listens to the responses, she establishes a positive relationship with her employees. When you, as the leader, take the time to talk to the person repairing equipment in the repair shop, the message comes through loud and clear: "I care about you and what you are doing." Employees recognize this attitude and tend to respond with increased loyalty and dedication.

Marine Example

I was a Corporal and this was in 1960 but I remember it like it was yesterday. The new Second

Lieutenant, Lt. McNally (I even remember his name), called me into his office and said, *"Cpl. Rose, I hear no one in the Company knows the M-14 like you do. Would you take some time and show me the way you field strip this weapon?"*

After I showed him the standard procedure for field stripping the M-14, he thanked me and then said, *"Now, can you show me your secrets? Can you show me the things that we shouldn't be doing with this weapon, but may need to do in the field? Show me what I need to look out for, and what might trip me up when I do this."*

We then spent several more hours together with me as the instructor. Through this exchange, the Lieutenant showed me that I had something to contribute to the unit, that what I knew mattered. He showed me he valued my opinion and expertise, and that made me want to do more for him.

John Rose
Corporal USMC
CFO
The Horst Group

Asking questions about what an employee is doing is worthless—*unless you care about the response.* Marine legend, Gen. Chesty Puller, put it simply: *"They won't believe you if you shoot bull."*

Technical expertise, as opposed to competence, can be a dangerous area for any leader, particularly a new one. One risk arises when a new leader tries to establish credibility by jumping in too often to lend a hand or to show he can do the work. A second emerges when the new leader's expertise overshadows his employee's ability to do the assignment in question. A third risk crops up when the leader is insecure about delegating. Let's take a look at examples of each of these.

Marine Example

I was a new platoon commander training in the field as part of a larger unit exercise. We were to conduct a raid, using small boats to get to the objective area. Time was limited. Only a few hours were available to plan the attack, brief the plan to all the participants, conduct rehearsals, and gather final intelligence updates prior to executing the mission.

A fairly common technique used in military operations at the platoon level is to create a terrain model of the area, which involves making a scale representation of the objective area out of dirt, sticks, cardboard, string, and anything else lying around, based on the topographic map and intelligence of the area. The mission brief is then conducted with people gathered around the terrain model to help participants visualize the operation and to familiarize them with the overall situation.

I issued initial orders and guidance to my platoon sergeant and squad leaders so they could make preparations. I then worked on my plan and began to build a terrain model. The platoon sergeant interrupted, asking if I wanted someone else to take care of the terrain model, so I could concentrate on developing my plan. I declined. The platoon sergeant further inquired, *"Are you sure this is the best use of your time, Sir?"* Again, I declined assistance.

After the raid, I sat down with the Company Commander to debrief the exercise. He noted that some details were lacking in the preparation of the mission. He said things looked chaotic as brief time approached. I explained my methodology and talked of building the terrain model. When pressed as to why I built the model, I answered that I wanted it to be right. The CO praised me for my desire for accuracy, but added, *"I know you know how to read a map, and I know you know how to build a basic terrain model. What you don't know is how to plan and execute a raid and that is what we are out here to do today. Next time, let one of your corporals make the terrain model."*

When I went back to debrief the platoon sergeant, I related the comment about the terrain model and how the sergeant had been right in trying to get me to delegate that responsibility. My demonstration of humility in that single exchange went a long way in insuring future success.

The sergeant smiled and walked me to a clearing a short distance away. There, on the ground, was a terrain model—much better than the one I had made. The sergeant explained that he had one of the corporals make it, in case I didn't have time to finish mine. I reflected on the hour I spent working on the model, and how that time could have been better used getting those details the Commander had talked about.

The sergeant told me, *"Sir, we trust you because you are the Lieutenant, and you wouldn't be in that position if the Corps didn't think you could handle it. You need to trust us, too. We want you to look good, but we can't help you look good if you are not doing what you are supposed to be doing. And we can't help you look good if you won't let us help you."*

I never built a terrain model again, and I learned to trust and delegate, to enable me to be more effective.

Steve Ripley
Captain USMC
Owner
Fawcett Boats

The second danger, that of a supervisor's skills outshining his employees, often shows up when that supervisor has been promoted to overseeing a function in which he is quite proficient. He might well find himself directing the same crew he was part of just the day before.

One of the biggest challenges in leadership starts with people who have technical competence but can't let go of what made them successful.

Ian Walsh
Captain USMC
Divisional Vice President
Fortune 100 company

Even more difficult is the situation in which the new leader still functions in a crew-member capacity part of the time, but exercises supervision over the crew the rest of the time-say, a working foreman position. Often, this individual has been placed in the supervisory position *because* of demonstrated proficiency at the task he is supervising.

Civilian Example

I was the Director of Operations for a commercial well-drilling company. We had a guy who was an artist with a drill rig. He knew how to finesse the bit down into the hole, and he was smart about all aspects of drilling. He was a natural. Well, we did what most companies would do; we promoted him to team leader. He was then supervising a drill crew of three or four people. He did fine working alongside the other three, setting the pace and taking immediate corrective action if one of his crew made a mistake.

We commended him for his ability to "make it happen," which reinforced his behavior of jumping in to fix mistakes. When we unexpectedly lost our General Superintendent, we made the hasty decision to promote this team leader into that newly vacated spot.

In this role, he oversaw several foremen who were running drill crews. Each time he visited a crew, he showed them the "right way to do it"—after all, he was the best driller in the company. But there was a problem: overall profitability was dropping. We were doing the same work, at the same bid margin, but we weren't making as much money. And the only thing that had changed was the guy in the General Superintendent position. Promoted from foreman, he was too busy *doing* the work, and not busy enough supervising and planning it—that is, *leading and managing*.

We coached him on the importance of *influencing* the foremen, but it was tough for him to let go of the controlling behavior that had made him successful and that the company had always rewarded him for.

To our credit, we were able to start a new crew and put him in charge of it. He was too good to lose and we had to help him save face. But, we failed in the first place by hoping he would make a good General Superintendent, just because he was a good driller.
Jeff Schade
Captain USMC
Consultant
National consulting firm

THE SUCCESS TRIANGLE

I demonstrate this concept with The Success Triangle. At the base of the triangle is technical proficiency. Knowing the job is the foundation of success. But to be successful as you are promoted, you need to become proficient in managing and leading, also.

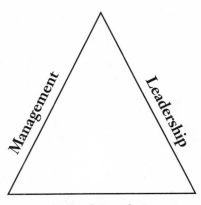

Technical Proficiency

In the example above, the driller failed to recognize the importance of learning the top two legs of the triangle. Instead, he continued to emphasize his technical expertise. His choice to leave his managerial and leadership skills incomplete (see diagram below) weakened his ability to effectively supervise his crews. His triangle collapsed.

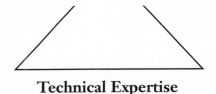

Technical Expertise

This situation is not limited to the field; it happens in the office, too. Consider the accounting supervisor who is known for her attention to detail. Nothing slipped by her when she was a clerk, and now, nothing slips by her as a supervisor because she practically replicates the work of her team as she checks and re-checks their work. She puts in longer hours, but that's what it takes to make the numbers right. Her people may not get it right, so she will make sure everything adds up.

Civilian Example

My college crew coach is a great example of what *not* to do. He knew his stuff. His rowing style was the most efficient I had ever seen and he was a great tactician. Individually, he was excellent. The university recognized his talent when they hired him to be the coach. But the guy had zero personality. Not an ounce of charisma, or anything else to make you want to work for him. He had one style: demand more. And I admit that, in making those demands, he made some of us better rowers. But he alienated us, too. There was nothing human about the guy. He was unapproachable. He made us better, yeah, but he could have made us *great*. He wanted perfection based *on his method*. No one could row as well as he, he thought. His style, if you could call it that, caused us to turn off our own motivation, creativity, and desire to excel. Further, he was unable to teach; all he could do was demand.

Rob Peterman
Major USMC

Civilian Example

We promoted one of our top salesmen to sales manager. We knew the pitfalls, but this was a smart guy who said he wanted the new challenge, and we were smart people who knew we could manage the situation—or so we thought.

He kept doing what he had always done; he didn't understand his new role. He was more interested in the *title* of Sales Manager than in working as the manager of a sales force. He preferred chatting on the phone with his old clients, shaking hands at trade shows, and making joint sales calls with junior sales people. The problem was that while he was doing these things, he was not supervising the performance of his team, nor was he holding them accountable for results. He wasn't even coaching his junior staff when he was at the trade show or on a joint call. He simply continued the behavior that had made him a successful seller.

His ego wanted to be the sales manager, but his heart was unable to make the change to the role of leader. He thought being in the leadership position meant more visibility and notoriety for him, and he was right. He didn't think about the change in behavior necessary to succeed in that position. After a lot of talking but no change in behavior, he was fired fourteen months later.

Kelly Caulk
Captain USMC
Account executive
International software company

The fundamental problem in each of these examples is that these newly appointed leaders failed to recognize they are no longer getting paid to *actually do the work*. They are getting paid to ensure the work gets done *by others*.

By insisting on doing much of the work themselves, they are failing to exercise supervision. They are not leading. They're still trying to be the best at what they *used to do*. They are not encouraging their team to grow, nor are they developing their own talents as a supervisor. This behavior creates several bad situations.

The first is poor morale. The vast majority of people pride themselves on doing a good job. They relish the opportunity to make a contribution. When a supervisor jumps in to "fix" a problem, he sends the message that he does not trust the employee to do the work correctly. This lack of trust causes the employee to mentally and emotionally "check out." Any chance he had to make an impact has been taken away. And what if there's a mistake? That's not a problem-the boss will rush in and "save the day."

Marine Example

I was an adjutant, trained by the Marine Corps to be an expert on administration and correspondence. I worked for a battalion Executive Officer. This guy was a perfectionist. What made things worse was that fifteen years earlier, he had served as an adjutant for a few months and thought he was an expert at the job.

I was responsible for all correspondence from the unit and wanted to represent the unit well. I took pride in my work and in every piece of correspondence my people created.

The problem was that my boss wanted everything done *his* way. I am not talking about Marine procedures; this was more about writing style. He would change "happy" to "glad" when he was reviewing correspondence. A few days later, he would change "glad" to "happy." Nothing I produced ever made it across his desk without being edited, bled on with red marker, and sent back for a re-write. It was demoralizing. No matter what I did, he would change it.

Knowing he was going to do this to everything I submitted, I stopped trying so hard. And I confess, for a time, the quality of my work really dropped. He didn't notice, since he was proofreading and changing everything anyway.

I was miserable. I wasn't proud of the product I was producing but it was hard to care, knowing nothing I did would be good enough for the Executive Officer. I eventually sought a transfer to get away from him. As it turns out, he left the unit before I did. My job performance and morale immediately improved.

Lisa Radnich
Lt Col USMCR
Physicians assistant

When the supervisor does the work, the subordinates lose the opportunity to train and grow. In the same breath with which supervisors lament that there are no good employees, they berate their own subordinates because they can't do the work as they are "supposed to." But how can the employee improve if the supervisor keeps jumping in to "help"?

If the supervisor is too busy redoing his team's work, then he is not using his time to carry out his own responsibilities. These may not be directly related to production, so they may not be missed initially. But they will be caught later, after the problem has snowballed. For example, the superintendent we saw earlier may be in charge of filling out time sheets. Half the time, he turns them in late, and the rest of the time, they are inaccurate. Payroll is now forced to track him down to correct the problem, driving down office productivity.

Additionally, this supervisor is holding himself back. By continuing to micro-manage his staff, he ensures that no one will be available to take his place. Therefore, he cannot advance. Some supervisors mistakenly think that, by not developing their subordinates, they are maintaining job security. In fact, what they're doing is hurting the company *and* themselves. This is an important point. Few companies do a credible job of articulating a compelling future for their employees. They either can't articulate it because they really don't know what it is, or they will not articulate it because they are afraid to share that information. The problem is that if employees don't know the next step for them they might get anxious and leave the firm, wrongly thinking there is no future there.

To overcome this problem, a company must provide the following: 1) a thorough description of the supervisory position, 2) strong leadership from those who oversee the new supervisor, 3) training for the newly promoted supervisor in management, leadership, efficient use of time, delegation, and profitability, and 4) a statement of why this person was selected for the position.

The pace of change today is rapid, and employees need to be doing what they are paid to do. Line employees need to produce; supervisors need to lead their employees in that production. Senior leadership should do everything possible to make sure those two groups have the training and resources to do their jobs the best they can. Senior leaders also need to look longer term, but they can do so only if all else is running smoothly.

SETTING THE STANDARDS

The Marines recognize the necessity for this evolution of skills as people get promoted. They address it in one of their fundamental doctrinal publications, *Warfighting: The early stages of a leader's career are, in effect, an apprenticeship. . . . This is where they learn their trades as aviators, infantrymen, artillery men, or logisticians . . . the goal at this stage is to become an expert in the tactical level of war . . . As an officer continues to develop, mastery should encompass a broader range of subjects and should extend to the operational level of war. At this stage, an officer should not only be an expert in tactics and techniques but should also understand combined arms, and amphibious warfare, and expeditionary operations. At the senior levels, an officer should be fully capable of articulating, applying, and integrating MAGTF (Marine Air-Ground Task Force) war fighting capabilities in a joint and multinational environment and should be an expert in the art of war at all levels.*

Marine example

I was working in the operations section of a Marine division. A battalion commanding officer returned after a very successful eighteen-month tour of duty overseas. During his time overseas, he was recognized as an expert in infantry operations. As testimony to his success at the battalion level, he was promoted to Colonel and became the Operations

Officer for an entire Marine Division. He was then charged with developing and executing operational plans for the Division—an organization nine times the size of a battalion and with a larger mission.

This role required that he take on a different perspective. He was responsible for all the assets of the Division: infantry, artillery, armor, and supporting units. He was also in charge of planning for and integrating supporting assets that were not part of the Division—such as aircraft. It was difficult for him to adapt to this new, broader view. His success as an infantry officer had been primarily due to his ability to analyze all the angles of a given situation—in detail, at the battalion level.

He was unable to apply this skill to the bigger picture. He couldn't articulate his concepts to his staff. When we didn't deliver what he wanted, he implemented his own solutions and told us to "make it happen." He wasn't considering the whole spectrum though. We routinely failed to order enough equipment to adequately support the Division because he told us we didn't need to; his plan was good. His plans had been good at the battalion level but at division he relied on old skills. He was soon relieved of this duty.

Anonymous

Technical competence of the leader also ensures that standards are maintained. In the absence of technical competence from the leader, the product, process, or service may be substandard, but the leader does not know it because he is not familiar enough with the output to make an appropriate evaluation. The standard must be maintained and leaders have a duty to ensure that it is. They can do so only if they understand the task. That means there must be some familiarity with the job. This familiarity may come from experience coming up the ranks, from a formal training program, or from walking around and asking questions. How it is developed is less important than the fact that it is developed. Again, though, we are looking for competence and not expertise.

Civilian Example

The company I worked for operated rail yards. One of our operations was losing money; I got the call to go fix it. The first thing I did was get out with the men to see what they were dealing with. I wanted to know the specifics of their situation so I could made good decisions.

Right from the outset I spent a lot of time familiarizing myself with my new team's responsibilities. This step is important because, first, I can only improve a situation if I understand it. Second, if I know the process, it is tougher for the men to take advantage of me.

For example, one old-timer told me it would take four hours to change a brake shoe, so the job would have to wait until next week, as it was only three hours until quitting time. I nodded, put on my coveralls and said, "I have some time; let's get it started." As luck would have it, the task was finished in just two hours. From then on, the men understood that I was aware of how long it takes to change a brake shoe (or whatever) and they were more inclined to complete the work in a timely manner.

Jon Hruska
Captain USMC
Group manager
National logistics company

Technical competence enables the leader to make accurate assessments and to assign the task to the most qualified person.

Civilian Example

I'm a fitness buff. I enjoy biking, running, kayaking, rock-climbing, etc. I wanted to stay close to my passion so I left a national consulting firm and opened a bike shop.

I don't have the bike maintenance knowledge that some of my employees do. They knew more about it than I did when I hired them—which is *why* I hired them—and they spend more time doing it. I know whether a bike is in tune or not, and I know when I need to ask for help. And I know whom to ask. I know enough about bike maintenance to perform some basic steps and to troubleshoot what is wrong so I can give a customer an estimate, but beyond that I leave it to my people. The ones who are getting paid for—and who know how to do—the work.

Dave Lane
Captain USMC
Owner
Patuxent Adventure Center

The issue of technical competence often presents itself in recruiting and promotion. In many firms, there is a strong bias against those who did not "come up through the ranks," particularly with operations and more task-oriented businesses. The error these firms make in their hiring and promotion process is in looking for technical *expertise* rather than technical *competence*. The most technically qualified person in the firm may not be the most qualified to lead people. Additionally, the company may be missing some outstanding talent from the outside who may be the exact people to take the firm to the next level.

The military addresses this issue with the rank of Warrant Officer. These Officers are expected to be technical experts in their given field and are recognized for this expertise. They come from the enlisted ranks and are highly respected and valued.

Some firms in corporate America have seized on this concept of recognizing the generalist and the specialist and have created career tracks for both. This approach is a positive way to nurture the careers of impact players and contribute to the long-term viability of the firm. It is not unusual to see this type of person in highly technical, often research- related, areas of expertise that require specialized education. For firms that have not made this adjustment, it is imperative that they clearly understand and communicate the expectations and requirements for advancement.

Civilian Example

I was hired by a national quick-service restaurant chain that began recruiting junior military officers (JMOs) in the mid-1990s. This was the result of a new CEO and new VP of Human Resources, both of whom had successfully hired new managers from the military in their previous firms. The established traditionalists in the company were strongly opposed to this new course of action. They argued that military men and women did not know the business, they were not suited for the job of Area Manager (overseeing five to fifteen restaurants), managers who worked for them would rebel, and the firm would experience high turnover at the critical unit manager level. Ultimately, hiring JMOs would be a disaster.

This resistance, however, didn't affect the decision to source from the military. To attract JMOs to the less-than-glamorous fast food industry, the firm recruited us aggressively and compensated us nicely.

A number of JMOs had just entered training and were attending a regional operations conference. We were not welcomed by the old-guard and little was done to make us feel at home, except by the training manager who was responsible for getting us ready to assume responsibility for an area.

The training manager laid out a training program that would take us through every crew position and all of the management functions at the unit level. We were to learn very specifically about all the tasks necessary to run a restaurant of this type successfully, as well as the standard for proficiency. We were assigned an area manager "running mate" to help with growth and development.

The scheduled six-month training program was nearly halved as a result of our rapid progress. As we finished training, the CEO met with each of us to explain his philosophy, vision, and expectations for us as new area managers. He assured us of his confidence, telling us, *"I hired you for your judgment."*

To establish credibility with our employees, we not only spent time in their restaurants, but we actually *worked* in the restaurants. We led by example, and we learned the basics of the jobs in the restaurants. We performed many of the "lower-ranking" jobs in the unit whenever it was necessary to fill a gap and insure high customer service. Additionally, we used all the leadership principles we knew. Very quickly, two things happened. First, managers and employees saw we were not afraid to get dirty and actually knew how to do the job. Second, the word spread. Managers compared notes and saw that this behavior was consistently applied. The boss really *did* know the fundamentals of the job and was confident about stepping in to help.

Also, we showed respect for those who did the job daily. When a new product was introduced, we learned about it first and then helped coach the rest of the team.

Many of us moved up to positions of increased responsibility and greater impact for the firm. The fears and arguments of the entrenched old-guard never materialized.
Wally Adamchik
Major USMCR
Consultant

This case is an excellent example of a company's knowing what it wanted in a candidate and understanding all the training required for the regional management role. This next example does not end as happily. In a situation much like the fast-food restaurant example, a JMO was heavily recruited by an oil-drilling and exploration company. He held an undergraduate degree in engineering as well as an MBA—both from fine schools. He joined the firm and was immediately sent to work on an oil rig as a roughneck. The company had a policy that all operations employees would have rig experience. The program was advertised as being of six-month to one-year duration, and it was strongly suggested that it would likely be closer to six months.

Civilian Example

I welcomed the opportunity to get to learn the technical aspects of the business. After six months of a rigorous one week on/one week off the rig work schedule, I met with the Vice President in charge of the training program and asked what was next on his development plan. The VP told me I would stay on the rig a bit longer. Again, I had no problem with this training program.

At the twelve-month mark, I met with the VP and again asked, "What's next?" He again told me, "Just a bit longer." This time I asked, "What specifically am I supposed to be learning?" and "What assignment can I look forward to upon completing the training program?" Unlike the restaurant company example, there was no plan, nor was there a list of the skills and behaviors which I was expected to become proficient in (or, at least, familiar with). The VP was unable to tell me anything except the party line, "We want our operations people to have rig experience." I asserted that a year on the rig might be enough, and if I knew what I was expected to learn during that year, I would be able to say that I had learned it, or I could then seek out the opportunities to learn that skill. Although being in the field for this long was starting to wear on me, the most frustrating part of the situation was that no one could articulate any plan for me as far as a future role within the company. They also changed the schedule from a one week on/one week off to a two weeks on/two weeks off schedule.

The VP responded with, "Just a bit more time on the rig." At the fourteen-month mark, I again spoke with the VP. Same conversation, same answer. I promptly resigned.

Tom Matkin
Major USMCR
Professional engineer

The lost opportunity for the employee and for the firm in this example is difficult to calculate. Each of them had invested fourteen months of time and money, yet neither enjoyed any positive return on these investments. The Old School thinking about the need to "know the business," unsupported by clear direction on just what constitutes technical proficiency, insured a negative outcome in this situation. Of course, the employee could not learn everything about rig operations in one year, but it is even more certain that he could not learn it in the absence of a clear training program and a desired standard of technical competence.

SUMMARY

Successful leaders know and understand the jobs they supervise. They are able to make decisions based on that knowledge, thereby increasing their credibility. Successful organizations recognize the new skills and responsibilities necessary for continued success at higher levels, and they work to put qualified people into those positions of greater impact and responsibility.

The willingness to "get dirty" once in a while demonstrates respect for the people being led. It enables the leader to understand the conditions the employees face and to craft strategies to help them succeed. The leader who knows the requirements of the tasks is better able to troubleshoot when things go wrong and to help employees. Competence also enables leaders to know how to detect when they are being told the whole story.

The issue of technical competence vs. technical expertise is critically important. Yet, it is one that many senior executives fail to grasp. The most effective leaders are able to balance this approach. It is a fine line, but one worth walking.

The executive should not be deeply involved in the tactics. Awareness and understanding of them is important, but senior leaders need to be focused on the big picture while trusting juniors to execute.
Verne Nelson
Lt Col USMC (deceased)

End of chapter application for
individual consideration and group discussion

1. Are you technically competent at the tasks you supervise?

2. Are you a technical expert at the task you supervise? Does this present any opportunities in light of reading this chapter?

3. If you are a technical expert at the task you supervise, does this present any challenges after reading this chapter?

4. What do you need to stop doing to be more effective as leader? When will you make this change?

5. What do you need to start doing to be more effective as a leader? When will you start?

6. Does your firm recognize the difference between competence and expertise?

7. Think of someone who does a good job of walking this line. Discuss how he or she does it.

8. Think of someone who does not or did not do a good job walking this line. Discuss the consequences of that inability.

9. Do your training and development programs set clear objectives of targeted skill levels?

10. Do your subordinate managers understand the shift required from "doing" to "leading" as they advance in the future?

Set the Example

Inspiring Followers
Being a Role Model
Professionalism

The only way an officer can demonstrate his leadership qualities is through personal example . . . I for one have never believed that you should ask any person to do anything that you wouldn't do yourself.
General Lewis H. Wilson
quoted in Karel Montor et al.,
Naval Leadership; Voices of Experience, 1987

"Marines are already looking to you for a pattern and a standard to follow. No amount of instruction and no form of discipline can have the effect of your personal example."
Guidebook for Marines

You cannot lead people from behind your desk. When you do come out from behind the desk, there are several reasons you are doing so: to role-model proper behavior, to inspire and influence others, to be visible, and to enable direct communication. In Peters and Waterman's 1988 classic book, *In Search of Excellence*, this behavior is "management by walking around." The Marines have been doing it since 1775. Setting the example is one of the most often mentioned elements of good leadership.

A commonly offered definition of leadership from people is the theme of "accomplishing results through people doing things they may not normally want to do of their own accord." Setting the example is perhaps the most basic way that Marine leaders get these results. Skeptics will argue that all a leader in the military has to do is issue an order and the job will get done. Perhaps that is true, but will the job get done in the appropriate time and to the appropriate standard? The Uniform Code of Military Justice is the code of law that all American service members choose to live by. Contrary to popular belief, the military doesn't "just court martial them" if they don't do the work. Cases of direct insubordination are rare and are usually handled at some level below the court martial. Marines do what they are told because they are Marines and they believe in the mission. They know they cannot be fired if they don't do those things, but they still do them. Unlike most civilians who can be fired, it is tough to fire a Marine.

Employees do what they are told because they understand that to stay employed they must do those things, and they might be fired if they don't do those things. However, real leaders want their people to perform, not conform. The goal is to get high performance from people because they want to give it, not to extract compliance and conformance from people because the rules mandate their work.

Setting the example is one of the primary ways leaders begin to establish credibility and rapport with those they lead. Physical training (PT) is one of the most obvious and often cited ways a Marine leader sets the example. Most Marines are in good shape, but Marine leaders recognize the impact they have on the unit so they often try to be in better shape than their Marines. Those being led do not require their leader to be the fastest runner. They do want their leader to be near the front of the pack and they *expect* them to be delivering 100 percent effort. Beyond being a role-model giving 100 percent, by participating in PT with the Marines the message is being sent that, "I am in this with you; we are in this together. I respect you and what you do." Unfortunately, there are some officers and senior enlisted who always seem to have something else to do at PT time. And when they do PT with the unit, they are at the back of the pack. Obviously, the credibility and the effectiveness of these individuals is negatively impacted by this behavior.

Physical fitness is about more than success in combat. Health and wellness are integral parts of success in most endeavors. The strains of leadership are exacerbated in the unfit person. These magnified strains make it more difficult for the leader to think and act at the highest levels of effectiveness. The desire of the leader to remain fit, despite the time demands of most jobs, sends a positive message about balance and prioritization. For businesses to remain competitive, they need all employees operating at maximum capacity, efficiency, and effectiveness. In fact, best-of-class companies, like SAS, are known for their proactive approach to this area. Physical fitness is becoming a competitive advantage as health care costs escalate. The leader must set a good example in all areas.

The business reader of this book is correct in thinking that the PT example is less applicable in the civilian sector. However, there are countless ways, positively and negatively, in which you set the example every day. Physical training is a great way to introduce the concept, but let's look at some other examples that are more easily accomplished. Your appearance, the way you dress, your bearing, carriage and demeanor, for example. You set the example through your conduct, the way you treat other people, and the attitude you bring to work every day. Simply being enthusiastic and having passion for what you do go a long way. Conversely, your negativity can suck the life out of your work group. These are just a few ways you can set the example every day.

Inspiring Followers

This illustration is 100 percent true. Yet, it would be easy to fabricate such a story because every Marine has many stories like this.

Marine Example

It was August and it was hot. On the flight line (where all the aircraft are parked and where some maintenance is performed) at a Marine Corps Air Station it seemed even hotter as the sun beat down from above and the heat rose from the concrete. The effective temperature was well over 100 degrees. Proper procedures, such as water coolers on the flight line, mandatory breaks, and modified uniform, were in place to reduce the possibility of heat exhaustion.

One airplane had a problem that was proving difficult to solve. It was one of those situations in which each time one thing was repaired, another thing broke. The three Marines working on the airplane were frustrated, but they also took pride in being able to fix aircraft so they kept hard at work. They probably skipped a break or two when they were supposed to get inside and cool down.

I got back from a two-hour flight. Just to put this in perspective, I arrived at work at 6 AM to conduct mission planning, the two-hour flight brief went from 8 AM to 10 AM, now it was 1 PM and I was hot and tired. On my way to the hangar I stopped for a quick talk with the Marines and went in to debrief the flight for an hour. Now 2 PM, after the debrief, I walked across the street to the convenience store and bought eight popsicles. I returned to the flight line at 2:30 PM and gave each Marine two pops and ate two myself (my first food since 5 AM) while we got into the shade, where it was still over 100 degrees. We talked a bit about the frustrations of the day working on the aircraft. They asked how my flight went and if my plane had any maintenance issues. There were none. After ten minutes I said, "Let's go take a look (at the airplane giving you trouble) and show me what you have done." Back in the sun, I again listened, asked some questions, and offered a thought or two (all of which the Marines had already tried, of course). I sincerely thanked them for working so hard and acknowledged the hot conditions. I offered encouragement that they would get it fixed and walked to the hangar.

For eight dollars and a few minutes in the sun I knew I would get an incalculable return on that investment in loyalty and effort from those Marines.

Now Wally, when you put that story in your book you make sure you are very clear that this story is about being out there with your people and caring. This story is not about what a great guy I am for spending eight bucks on ice cream. And what I did was nothing unusual; you know that any good leader would do the exact same thing.

John Brix
Major USMC
Airline pilot

John Brix wasn't born with the understanding that buying a popsicle from time to time was good leadership. He saw other leaders behave this way, and he made a conscious decision to set the example when he stepped into leadership roles. He knew the impact this behavior had on him when he was the subordinate, and he worked to make this part of his normal procedures.

Civilian Example

We were building a distribution facility on the outskirts of Dallas. It was the summer and it was hot, as you would expect in Texas. I was an assistant project manager on the job, which is a nice way of saying I pushed a lot of paper around. This assignment required that I get out to the job site every other week.

Our guys were working hard to get the project completed on time. I went to the job one Saturday and found several employees putting in some overtime. Since nobody was around, they weren't wearing all the proper safety equipment. I didn't know them very well. Things were normally so hectic on the job sites that I never had time to talk with any of our field people. Of course it was hot. So, mid-morning I put on my hard hat and safety glasses and walked over and told them I was running out for breakfast. I then told them it was "on me" and asked if they wanted anything. A couple of biscuits, a few beverages, and a bag of chips. Not much. When I returned we sat around for a half-hour and talked about the job and about each other. I shared that I had been in the Marines; one of the older hands had been a grunt in Vietnam. Another guy had kids the same age as mine.

Very quickly and easily I now had the beginning of a relationship with these guys. As we wrapped up the talk, I put my hard hat back on and made a comment about dressing for safety and they put all their safety gear on. From then on whenever I was on the job, we would exchange a few kind words, and from then on it seemed whenever I needed things or help from the field guys, I always got it. And when I was around I never had to talk to these guys about safety either.

John Hayes
Major USMCR
Project manager
Regional construction company

Setting the example is not conditional; it is an all-the-time behavior. The way we apply the principle may differ but the principle is constant. When the stakes are high and the risks great, the principle applies to an even greater degree. The pressure and stress of combat are unlike any other human endeavor, yet people go to war. Often that willingness to remain steadfast in combat and the adherence to standards in the face of difficult conditions are the results of solid leadership. Leaders set the example through physical courage and, more important, moral courage—doing the right things.

Marine Example

General Mattis was always there, or so it seemed. He regularly held meetings with his commanders right behind the front lines. This habit reduced miscommunication and it was also great for morale. Let's face it; the General didn't need to be up front, practically in mortar range. The Marines learned about it and they knew they were not alone, they knew they were being heard and thought of because the guy who made the decisions was out there with them.

Let me add another comment on setting the example. In combat I think there is a tendency to lower the standard when it comes to conduct, behavior, and human nature. However, the norms and standards must be adhered to even more so in that situation. We had a few cases with Marines not following the proper sanitation procedures because they were in a combat zone. Every single leader from junior enlisted to senior officer needs to work to change the erroneous perception that the standards change in a combat zone. We do so by role modeling, explaining and disciplining when necessary.

Here is why it matters. Today you may decide not to shave, or you may urinate where you are not supposed to. What then will stop you from not cleaning your weapon tomorrow, and then firing indiscriminately into a crowd of civilians the next day? We need to maintain standards. It is not very different in the civilian sector. When I go to Burger King I have a certain expectation. If a restaurant is having a hard time hitting its numbers, a manager may be tempted to cut back a bit on labor or on food portions. I may recognize that something isn't right and not come back, or the entire crew may interpret this cutting of corners differently. One crew member may not put the right amount of lettuce on my burger, and the next one, knowing the store manager has low integrity, decides it is OK to skim a few bucks out of the cash till. Where does it stop?

Set the right example to help your people understand and live the norms of conduct.
Ken Maney
Lt Col USMC

The behavior of General Mattis is not some affectation reserved for military leaders. Corporate leaders at all levels can, and should, be out front. Lindsay Owen-Jones, the CEO of L'Oreal since 1988 put it this way in Fortune magazine in July 2004. *"When you have spent a day tramping from morning to evening, and from store to store, eating sandwiches in a minibus as you go from one place to another, you are sending an unwritten message to teams everywhere in the world that the CEO is doing the same thing he expects them to do—which for all us is to avoid living in some sort of ivory tower and to listen to our customers."*

BEING A ROLE MODEL

The Learning Channel carried a show called, "Now Who's The Boss." It featured senior executives from various companies working front line positions. Larry Flax and Rick Rosenfeld, co-chief executives at California Pizza Kitchen, participated and their comments are informative: *We thought it would be good for the morale of our people in our restaurants, and it was . . .we learned again how tough it is to do what our people do.*

Job exchanges need not be limited to television events. These create a powerful opportunity to increase mutual understanding in the organization and to deepen the respect and trust that are the bedrock of successful firms.

Civilian Example

An industrial laundry is not the most glamorous setting in the work world, but it does attract people who want to make a decent wage and to be treated with respect. And a lot of those people are women. One of the best things I could ever do was take time out and walk the floor and interact with them.

If I took the time to know them, and allowed them to know me, it sent a message that we are all human and all have issues to deal with outside of work. When I noticed a new haircut on one of the ladies, for example, the other 150 knew that I noticed before the shift was over. This courtesy validates them as people and it also shows that I pay attention. If they know I am paying attention, they are motivated to do the task correctly.

One of the most enjoyable things we did was to select somebody to be "boss for a day" while I would go perform their job. Talk about walking in someone else's shoes. It gave the employees a real sense of all of the things I did as a facility manager. It also gave me a chance to rotate through the different jobs. People respect you when you stand next to them on the line and make a sincere effort for eight hours. It is another way of reinforcing how important they are. And while I am on the line, not only am I learning but I am taking the time to do the job as perfectly as I can to communicate the standards we are supposed to deliver.

The key point is that my walking the floor wasn't a task to be done from time to time and checked off my to-do list; it is part of being an effective leader today. Any chance I had to be out on the floor and influencing people was well worth it, especially early on. Once they got to know me, it was less important for me to make the rounds from a process improvement point of view and more important from a morale point of view. Leaders can't lead if they are not seen.

Jeff Schade
Captain USMC
Consultant
National consulting firm

Here, Jeff was incorporating this behavior into his routine. In fact, this is easily done by simply scheduling time on your planner for it. However, there will be occasions when there is no time to plan or really think about the action required. These instances reveal the true nature of leaders.

Civilian Example

I am the Division Manager of a Fortune 100 company. I have a lot of people who report to me, and I am responsible for a lot of revenue. If my Division doesn't do well, the company doesn't do well. We manufacture low-tolerance parts for mechanical applications. We are talking microns here.

Cleanliness is important for us. From the minute you drive onto the campus where our facility is, you notice how well-kept the place is. When you enter our front office, the floors are shined, and when you walk onto the plant floor you think that surgery could be performed right then and there. It is that clean.

I was visiting this plant one afternoon while they were working hard to make an important delivery for us. The customer had placed a rush on some material, and we were jumping through hoops to get it out the door. Everyone was hard at work and all I was trying to do was stay out of the way. In the midst of this controlled chaos comes the crew that handles document storage for us. Every couple of months they come and move older material to an off-site location, pretty standard stuff.

As one of this crew is rolling his hand-truck with four document boxes stacked on it, he backs into a pillar and all four boxes fall. Their contents are on their way to making the place look like Times Square on New Year's Eve with confetti. You get the picture.

Several of us are watching this happen as if in slow motion and we are all frozen. This paper is going to spread everywhere and throw us off schedule. As the contents of one are about to get caught up in the quick moving air in the plant, I take off my suit jacket and throw it on top of the box. I then grab a fire blanket and throw it on top of the second box. I wasn't so lucky with number three and four. That paper was on its way to everywhere in the plant, and I started hopping around picking up paper. I didn't give any orders—which would have been easy—I just started working. And of course, so did everyone else. We got it all picked up in a few minutes. Without fast action we might have been shut down for an hour.

One of the plant foremen later told me that he came back from break and saw me hopping around and didn't know whether to laugh, run, or start picking up. He told me he had never seen any executives from our company do anything remotely like that. He said they would have let the "worker-bees" clean the mess up and probably miss the shipping deadline. The thought of one of the execs "getting dirty" was outside his frame of reality. But he then looked me straight in the eye and said, "If it is that important to you, then I will make sure all of my guys know it, and we will make it important to us. We won't let you down."

Anonymous
Major USMC
Division manager
Fortune 100 company

Setting the example is not only about giving your followers a proper role-model to follow; it gets to that deeper theme that runs through much of this book, respect. Your behavior and actions directly influence people. At its core, leadership is about influence. Influence can be exercised by people at any level in the organization. Influence is not limited to the CEO. In fact, some of the best examples of leadership are from people who have no positional power or authority but who are expected to get a job done—an external consultant assisting with a process improvement implementation, for example. Therefore, setting the example is a cornerstone of leadership.

Leaders need to be aware of their presence in front of a group. Many people are afraid to act proactively today because of some poor treatment from a previous boss. I call this the "whipped puppy syndrome." Even after years of being in a good home, a dog that was raised in an abusive home will cower as you raise your hand to pet it. It is no different with people. They may not physically cower but inside they are waiting for the blow.

I was working at a national consulting firm and one of the new consultants remarked to me after a few months, "I keep waiting for the other shoe to fall; this is too good to be true. Is this place really as good as it seems?" I replied that it really was and that he needed to get used to it if he was going to be truly successful. He had been micromanaged and continually belittled in a previous environment, and that is what he was expecting to happen in the consulting firm. What you do as a leader will have an impact, positively or negatively, for years to come.

PROFESSIONALISM

Setting the example is also about self-control. We want our leaders to be calm, cool, and collected under pressure. We want them to be professional. Whether that pressure is due to having to "take the hill" or to give the speech at the annual meeting, leaders need to display confidence. When they are uncertain and out of control, the followers are uncertain and the leader loses credibility. One of the Marines interviewed related that *"I finally learned to control my temper when I became the Aviation Maintenance Officer for a squadron that was underperforming. I had over 200 Marines looking at me. If I was shook up, they were going to be shook up."* His realization of the impact his behavior had on his people was an important part of the subsequent improvement in the readiness of that unit.

With the erosion of decency in society there has been an increased acceptance of profanity. From television to bumper stickers we are not surprised, nor shocked, anymore when we hear it. Yet this issue was noted by many interviewed.

The rough and tumble nature of the Marine Corps is indisputable. However, this environment does not offer carte blanche to use profanity. This issue has to do with standards of conduct, respect for the individual, and self-control.

Marine Corps Recruit Depots are the epitome of the Marine Corps experience. There is no denying that Parris Island and San Diego are unlike any other boot camp experience in America's military. And when you talk with the men and women who are charged with molding new Marines, it is clear they recognize the importance of setting the example. Jimmy Lane, Captain USMC, a series commander (overseeing three recruit platoons) at Parris Island, puts it this way: *educated people do not use profanity. We need to set the standard here. Sure, it might be different out in the fleet, but here we want to establish good muscle memory. We train correctly. There is no need for good leaders to lower themselves to the lowest common denominator.*

This is not a lone opinion. It is echoed by Marines at all levels of instruction and leadership at boot camp. They all recognize the impression they are making.

Marine Example

Drill Instructors put in 80–110-hour weeks here and are happy to do it. Yet, they are so aware. It is almost scary what they pick up on. In the middle of a thirty-minute conversation one of my Staff Sergeants may really pick up on one thing I said. He understands everything in our conversation but this one thing becomes huge. It might be a comment about cleanliness, it might be a bit of praise for him or one of his peers, it might even be a minor point of correction, but he picks up on it and it gets passed along and magnified. If it was good, it becomes great. If it was bad, it becomes horrific. My point is that we underestimate our impact as leaders, yet we need to be totally aware of the example we are setting, at all times. I am a Lieutenant Colonel now, and I still remember a few things that my Colonel told me when I was a Lieutenant twenty years ago. This care with words is a guiding principle for me. The profanity issue is about self-control and it is about abuse. The moms and dads of America send us their sons and daughters. We have to treat them correctly and that means treating them with respect. Do we slip sometimes? Sure, but it is a very rare exception, and we aggressively investigate and take corrective action.

Pat Campbell
Lt Col USMC

Setting a standard of excellence is about eliminating the acceptance of the status quo. That means things have to change but change doesn't need to be painful. Change certainly can't be well-implemented by decree. Leaders desiring change must model the behavior and generate the support of their people to accomplish real change.

Civilian Example

Our new manager was faced with taking over a division that was ranked eight of eight in the nation. His assessment was fast and candid. He pulled no punches in telling us the organization was too casual in its daily operations, that there was no accountability and that it was going to change.

In addition to some policy changes, he immediately got rid of business casual and instituted fines for people swearing. That got our attention. This guy was not some puritanical manager; he was human and fallible, like any of us, but he recognized the need to tighten things up, starting with the management team. We needed to elevate the level of professionalism in the division and it was going to start with us.

Every morning at the staff meeting he would place a large jar in the center of the table, and anyone who crossed the line on language had to throw in one dollar. All of us, including him, made a number of contributions to the jar. But he made his point, too.

If we expected the entire group to perform differently, then we had to start acting differently. Words are hollow and have no meaning unless backed up with actions. The change in dress and vocabulary was immediate and visible. Actions were backing up words and we got the unit turned around quickly.

I realized the turnaround was about more than making the numbers. Looking back on it, that new manager jumped in the fight with us. In doing so he showed us he was human *and* showed us we could do what he was asking. He made some mistakes. Let's face it; we are all human. We will make some mistakes but that doesn't mean we stop striving to improve. In fact, in the striving perhaps the best example is set: The example to remain focused and committed to the cause.

SethHensel
Captain USMC
Production manager
National manufacturing company

As change agents, leaders communicate in so many ways. The oft talked about but rarely used "open door" policy is another opportunity for you to show people what you believe. Recognizing that communication is essential to an effective organization, many bosses have some type of open-door policy, on paper. The reality is that when an employee wants to talk, the boss is often unavailable. Even worse is the boss who is available but uninterested. It doesn't take long for people to get the message that the door may be open but the mind of the person behind the door isn't.

Marine Example

Yes, I have an open-door policy and I pay a price for it. I am willing to pay that price. My Marines can come see me at any time. They have my home phone number, they have my office phone number, they have my email and they have a standing invitation to come talk to me. The reality is that in a squadron of a few hundred people I don't get calls and interruptions every day, but certainly once a week I get that drop-in visitor. And yes, I drop what I am doing and come out from behind my desk and sit with the Marine and we talk. Sometimes I may sense it is more than a casual visit, and I ask if we can schedule a better time, but I never blow them off.

My credibility is at stake. I told them I would be there for them. If I am not, they will not be there for me. Pretty simple. They need to know they have an advocate and someone to listen to them. By having a real "open-door" policy my entire squadron knows, because they can see it, that there is open communication. Good communication is so important in leading a complex organization. I can't make good decisions if people are not talking to me.

I have a sign on my desk that has a shark with a ghost busters circle through it—it stands for "no sharks." I call the Marines sharks if they lurk outside my door waiting for me to look at them versus just walking into my office. I have, on occasion, also referred to myself as "The Chaplain." It's amazing how many Marines just need someone to talk to, and, more importantly, listen to them. I surely don't have all the answers, nor am I that wise or intelligent, but if you treat people like people it's amazing the results you'll get. Loyalty and strong interpersonal relationships go a long way towards mission accomplishment.

Mike Finley
Lt Col USMC

Civilian Example

Do I really have an open door? I think so. I have seen places where the boss said it, but he never seemed to have time for anyone. When they come to my door with that questioning look on their face, and they see that I have a desk full of paper and two phones to my head, but then I drop everything and stand up and greet them, they know the open door is real. I welcome them in and we talk. We work to fix their problem. If someone complains of being shorted on pay, I call payroll and we look into it, right away.

I may give up some time when that happens, but I gain happy employees, and that is worth it.

Jon Hruska
Captain USMC
Group manager
National logistics company

SUMMARY

Setting the example is not about being perfect, nor is it about acting one way in public and another in private. It is about taking action to support the words you say. It is about giving your people an example of what you expect. It is far easier for me to imitate something I see rather than something someone tells me.

Setting a positive example is not a difficult thing to do. It may mean as leaders we need to move slower to make sure we don't skip any steps, but the message is so important. The message is that we are in this together, and I want you to do your job correctly, and I want you to do it well. Inspiration, trust, respect, role modeling, and composure are all components of setting the example. Do these and you will be exercising one of the key principles of effective leadership.

Don't confuse putting on a show with real substance. Colonel Stephen Oren, USMC retired, put it this way: *the rah rah stuff is fine but you still have to walk your talk. You must be in front of your people showing them the standard of excellence you expect. Don't just talk about it, do it. Show them.*

At The Basic School as a new Lieutenant I even learned a few phrases in Latin. Semper Fidelis, of course, but another was Ductus Exemplo— Leadership by example.

Al "Ziggy" Ziegler
Captain USMC (deceased)

End of chapter application for individual consideration and group discussion

1. Where in your work are you able to set the example?

2. Where at your work can your boss be setting an example?

3. Are the standards of conduct clear at your work?

4. Are there opportunities to discuss the importance of modeling the proper behavior with those in leadership positions?

5. Describe a time someone you looked up to did something to cause you to lose confidence in him or her. Why did you lose confidence? Did that person ever regain your confidence?

6. Describe a time when someone you worked for behaved in such a way that you still remember that person as a positive influence on you.

7. Do you take time to think about the impact your actions may have on someone five years in the future?

8. What are the risks of not thinking about the implications of your behavior?

9. Do your people have a clear picture of what the desired behavior is?

10. What methods of communication are you using to set the example?

Self-Awareness

Know Thyself
Personal Style
Situational Awareness

People are afraid of a leader who has no sense of humor. They think that he's not capable of relaxing, and as a result of this there is a tendency for that leader to have a reputation for pomposity, which may not be the case at all. Humor has a tendency to relax people in times of stress.
General Louis H. Wilson
Quoted in Karel Montor et al.,
Naval Leadership; Voices of Experience, 1987

Never stop learning. We should always look for ways to do things better and that looking starts inside ourselves.
John McNulty
Captain USMC
Division Manager
Fortune 500 company

You cannot lead anyone if you cannot lead yourself. Effective leadership of self depends on a high degree of self-awareness rooted in honesty and introspection. As individuals advance in their careers, they are exposed to new challenges and the opportunity to make decisions with the benefit of wisdom gained over time. However, this wisdom must be cultivated. It lies within all of us but only surfaces when it is sought. Not only do we as individuals face new challenges as we advance but society also throws challenges at us. Fortune magazine put it this way: *Leading a company today is different from the 1980s and '90s, especially in a global company. It requires a new set of competencies. Bureaucratic structures don't work anymore. You have to take command and control types out of the system. You need to allow and encourage broad-based involvement in the company.*

Stephen Covey in *The 8th Habit: From Effectiveness to Greatness* says, "The industrial age was about control, and the information age, or knowledge-worker age, is about release."

A logical extension of self-awareness is the style the leader uses to lead in this changing world. There are many labels to describe leadership styles. Some of these labels are authoritative, participative, charismatic, task-oriented, people-oriented, big-picture focused among others. Stereotypes fail us here. There is no one single leadership style that is most effective, in our society or in the Marines. All of the various styles can be effective or ineffective. The most important aspect of style is the ability to adapt it to be of maximum effectiveness. The most successful leaders are able to modulate and moderate their approach. A leader may use a different style for different people or choose a different style for a person given a different situation.

The recognition of their own styles and the situations they are operating in differentiates average leaders from superior leaders.

KNOW THYSELF

Leadership can be a heady experience. All of a sudden you are in charge. In fact, Adamchik's First Law of Leadership applies here: **it is all about you**. You must make the conscious choice that you accept the role of leader, formally or informally conferred by the organization. You accept the responsibility of leadership and recognize that you are in a special role. People look to you for guidance and for answers: they are depending on you. But if you are not careful, you begin to believe that the organization revolves around you. People are counting on you, after all, and the company thought highly enough of you to put you in this position of leadership, so you must be pretty good, or so you think. And you probably are good at what you do, but leadership is more about getting *others* to be good at what they do so that the entire group achieves its goals.

The problem here is that would-be leaders get stuck on the First Law of Leadership and never make it to Adamchik's Second Law of Leadership: **it is all about them**. Once you decide that you will be a leader and accept the requirements that go with it, everything you do after that must be focused on "them." Them being the ones we lead. This shift in thinking is one many fail to make, and this failure dooms them to a career of mediocrity. Leaders who accept the Second Law take a big step toward engaging the workforce. With this engaged workforce supporting them, they achieve great success. Admittedly, success as a leader requires more than an engaged workforce, but it is far more difficult to achieve without the workforce on your side.

One of my biggest frustrations is that it seems that only in reflection did I actually "get-it." I am better at seeing the learning as it is happening now, but I wish I had been more aware of it earlier in my career.
Ken Maney
Lt Col USMC

Marine Example

You can't hide from yourself. Most Second Lieutenants are pure. They are still idealistic. Some of them are arrogant because of the rank, but I think most are just happy to be there making a contribution. But then they get out of initial training and are out in the Fleet Marine Force where there are a lot of enlisted people, and they are all saluting you, all saying "Sir" or "Ma'am," and responding to your every word. Somewhere along the way you begin to believe the world starts and ends with you. It is hoped that you get through that stage quickly.

As a Captain I started to lose some of "me," and by my fourth boat ride (six-month cruise), as a Major, I was all attitude with all the answers. I was taking myself way too seriously. I then worked for a General who set a fine example and who really helped me to understand things. He mentored me in every sense of the word. And things started to change for me. Life, and command, got easier as I regained perspective.

I became me again. Self-assured, not arrogant. Inquisitive, not questioning. Respectful, not condescending. Aggressive, not overbearing. I became the things good Marine Officers are supposed to be when they have it all in proper perspective.
Eric Buer
Lt Col USMC

Eric is explaining what is often called authenticity. The follower wants the leader to be genuine. Genuine leaders are most effective because they truly know themselves. Honest self-assessment leads to self-confidence, humility, and respect for others. These qualities lead to congruence between what leaders say and what they do.

Being open to feedback is critical here. Usually, there are people trying to guide us in the right direction. All too often, however, leaders do not hear the feedback, and if they do, they rationalize that the person giving them the feedback doesn't really understand their situation. However, in those times when we listen we find the opportunity for growth.

Civilian Example

After work one night several of us went out for dinner. One of the more senior guys who had been around awhile remarked something like "Kevin, you can be kind of intimidating to some folks around here." We all laughed a bit but I had trouble sleeping that night.

The next morning I asked some people I trusted if they thought I was intimidating, and they all said I certainly could be. I asked for examples, and they explained that I liked to be close to people physically when I talked to them. Also, I had a tendency to talk *at* people, not *with* them. My body language tended to be closed. I thanked them for the feedback. I then asked for their help in pointing out times when I was communicating in a positive manner and in a negative manner.

This approach was very effective. First, people were shocked that I would even ask for their input. Second, they were surprised I asked for their help. These two responses by themselves made me less intimidating but I took real action. The bank offers all kinds of classes on things like effective communication and conflict resolution and I took them. These courses made me much more aware of my actions and my impact on people.

Several promotions later, I guess it is working. But I have also been reminded with these promotions that we always need to be learning new skills. Each new job is an opportunity, and I can make the most of the opportunity only with an open mind.

Kevin Baggott
Lt Col USMCR
Vice President
Fortune 100 financial services company

The true student of leadership moves beyond anecdotal stories and experiential development into the academic. By academic, I mean a lifelong study of the art and science of leadership. They seek to learn from others outside their normal frame of reference. This learning may come from talking with others, reading business books, reading academic research, or taking higher level classes. As an organization, the Marine Corps embraces this concept. The Corps regularly seeks input from experts outside the Corps and seeks to learn from them. A Marine Officer doing an exchange tour for one year with Home Depot is an example. The point is that Marines recognize the fluid nature of leadership and the necessity to stay sharp. According to Hunt and Phillips (1991), *"leaders are embedded in a dynamic, changing, environment and they must be able to assume different, contradictory, or competing roles at different times and in different situations."*

The concept of the study of leadership, and management, is difficult for many business leaders to embrace. This is a fundamental failure in violation of Adamchik's First Law: **it is all about you**. The simple fact is that people often have been promoted because of technical competence and do not recognize the need to become a student of leadership, as they are of their specific craft. Yet their now primary responsibility is the accomplishment of work through others. The fact is they are now spending a significant amount of their time in supervisory activities, but they are not investing the time to get better at them. They may think "I have arrived" or they may perceive themselves too busy. But in making these excuses they are saying they are not really interested in their group performing at a higher level. Some might consider this a harsh sentiment, but those with self-awareness and willingness to learn will not.

One of the factors that naturally surfaces in conversations about leadership is power. Here, as in most discussions on leadership, there are many nuances and variables. Power cannot be ignored, yet the most successful leaders rarely wield that power directly. One of the comments for this book came from a Marine General who said, "if you choose to raise your voice, you really don't know how to use the power you have." The status conferred by rank, or position, yields a certain amount of power, and that power will cause people to follow. Just because someone occupies a position of leadership does not mean he or she will be a good leader. In fact, we all know examples of people low in the hierarchy who wielded considerable power. But what is the source of that power? Ultimately, power comes from personal attributes and position in the organization. The amount of power one has is the sum of those two sources. Organizational power most often is sourced in the role you occupy, the resources you control, your access to and control of information, your personal network, and your reputation. Personal power is based on knowledge, ability to communicate, character, attraction, and past history. A student of leadership will learn the sources. A self-aware leader will seek to *understand* the sources and how to leverage them for the good of the group.

Marine Example

I am learning just as much today as a Lt Col as I was nineteen years ago as a Second Lieutenant. My ability to keep an open mind is essential. If I see myself ruling out options too quickly, I double-check to make sure I am being open.

With that said, core values do not change. But everything else around us in the world is changing. The attitude that "I still have a lot to learn" is mandatory for future leaders. Part of that learning process is to know, and admit, what I don't know. Society is changing, people are different, and I need to adjust. Certainly the junior needs to adjust to the senior. Nonetheless, my job as the senior is to reach all of my people, which means I probably have to change also.

Leaders need to be careful about the impact they make—which means they have to know what that impact is. I may see something going wrong but I may have to restrain myself from jumping in to fix it. If I open my mouth, it becomes a priority for the unit even if it is a small issue. Maybe the best impact I can have is to let it go and let people learn from it. Maybe the best impact I can have is to let it go so when I do have to jump in my people listen instead of mumbling "here he is again." When the senior leader gets too involved, he stymies creativity. The unit may do exactly what the leader wants, and it may accomplish exactly what the leader said he wanted, but if the unit is constantly responding only to the leader's standards, the unit will not perform in excess of that standard.

If I am focused on myself and not the unit, I will never see the possibilities in front of us. Tunnel vision yields marginal results. But when I maintain focus on the mission and on the people actually doing the work, I am more effective. Keeping it all in proper perspective is important, and that starts with knowing myself and working to become a better leader.

Pat Campbell
Lt Col USMC

Many supervisors today have been exposed, and sometimes subjected to, some type of psychometric assessment. They are known by names such as DISC, Myers-Briggs, Human Patterns, CPQ, Highlands Battery, and many others. These assessments are tools to help people be more effective on the job. They first do this by giving us a better understanding of ourselves. Then we are able to look at how we interact with others. These tools also help us understand others. Brewing giant SABMiller uses psychometric assessments in hiring and in major promotions to make sure people fit their culture. There are many of these tools, ranging from short and simple to long and complex, but they share a similar purpose of helping us become more effective through a higher level of self-awareness. Some assessments measure preference, some measure aptitude, others measure attitude, and some measure intelligence. Intellect, as we commonly know it (IQ) and emotional intellect (EQ) are measurable, with much being made of EQ lately. Traditional intelligence (IQ) is about knowledge and information. Emotional intelligence (EQ) is about knowing who you are, your empathy, your ability to reflect on self, and your impact on others. It is a much less tangible kind of intellect but a very important one.

A great leader has the full range of IQ/EQ and multiple styles and is, therefore, able to adapt. A good leader, on the other hand, has less range and is correspondingly less effective. But we can always get better at leading by more fully understanding our range and working to expand it.
Ian Walsh
Captain USMC
Divisional Vice President
Fortune 100 company

The internet has made many of these assessments widely, and cheaply, available. An important point here is to know what you are looking for before you start cranking through assessments. They are wonderful tools when used properly. Assessments contribute to self-awareness. They may confirm something we already knew or suspected, or they may identify something we did not know. Further, they help us coach others. But they are effective only when understood and applied. Acting on what you learn about yourself, and others, is the key.

Marine Example

Anybody who knows me and reads this will think I am joking but it is true. The Trish you saw as a child and even today in the crowd is an act. In my youth I got tired of people asking me "what's wrong" because I was not bouncing off the walls with the other kids. So, I started bouncing like the rest of them.

Then as I was getting out of the Marines as part of my transition plan I took the Myers-Briggs and I got the big "aha." I am an introvert. Big crowds do not recharge my batteries. It was like, all of a sudden,

I had permission to be me. Once I understood the introvert part, I could then make adjustments to my behavior in order to be more effective.
Trish Gibson
Lt Col USMCR
Federal law enforcement

Trish gives a fine illustration about the proper use of assessments. With the recognition that she is an introvert, she moved to smaller, often one-on-one, meetings with her work group because larger groups were uncomfortable for her. There are other things she can do, but she would not have been able to do any of them without this information. Armed with this better understanding of self, she can better lead. But this information is only part of the equation for effective leadership and can be a drawback.

Civilian Example

There are a lot of assessments and models on the market today: Situational Leadership, DISC, One-Minute Manager, FISH, Cheese. I have read them all and been through training on a bunch of them. And there is a lot of good information in them but let's not overdo it. You don't need to break the book out and consult the personality profiles every time you make a decision.

In learning any material there needs to be some flexibility because many of us learn differently. I like to take information home and chew on it for awhile. I realize this now, but early in my career bosses wanted me to speak up more in meetings. I knew what worked for me, but it may not have been consistent with their picture of success, so it was a problem. I learned, though, what works best for me, and now, rather than not say anything, I will participate and say I need to think about it.

Many organizations do a lot of training, using the various models and assessments, but at the end of the day all they did was talk about the material. Where is the action? They confuse talking about style with really understanding style and using the training to yield higher productivity. That is exactly the opposite of what these assessments are trying to get us to do. At some point we need to get past analysis and take action. The leader has to have the wherewithal to stand up and get the group moving.

Assessments are one component of self-awareness. They give part of the picture but there is more and we continually need to look for it within ourselves.

John McNulty
Captain USMC
Regional manager
Fortune 100 company

Beyond self-assessments, we should also consider the assessments of those who know us. Consider 360-degree feedback, the process whereby an individual is evaluated by seniors, peers and subordinates. This is an excellent tool that helps a leader improve. In this next example, watch the positive impact of a return to authenticity.

Civilian Example

I had been out of the Marines for several years and was back in the family business. I attended a program at the Center for Creative Leadership for a week and part of it was a 360 feedback session. Prior to the course I asked a number of people at work to evaluate me—pretty standard and I didn't expect much out of it. But when I got the feedback I was floored.

Basically they told me I was impersonal, that I was "all business." They didn't think too much of my technical skills or my leadership skills, either. I recognized that I was the son of the owner of the firm and I was playing that role. I was not being myself, and I certainly wasn't practicing the day-to-day leadership skills that I had learned in the Marines. I wasn't doing what I am naturally good at.

The corrective action was easy; I stopped playing the role and became me. I started saying hello, I talked to people in the halls, I laughed and smiled. After that, things just got a lot better at work, for everybody. And now as the President of the company I do the same thing. I think a few people thought I might become "presidential" as in "aloof." I contend that I am "presidential" as in "human."

John Russell
Captain USMC
President
Russell Construction Services

Good leadership recognizes the personal catwalk and the brutal self-assessment that is required to be effective. As a leader, I must understand who I am and what my style is to be effective. I have to take into account my own personal catalog of competencies, preferences, and style to be most effective.

Steve Ripley
Captain USMC
President
Fawcett Boats

PERSONAL STYLE

Your effectiveness is not solely a factor of what style you employ. It is not based on your natural instincts or on learned traits. Most researchers in organizational development agree with this point of view. David Segal, in *Military Leadership*, writes that "the nature and quality of the interaction between the leader and the other group members is a strong determinant of the effectiveness of the group." Yet we naturally want to know what style more often delivers interactions of the highest nature and quality? Of course, the answer is that any style can be effective. The biggest determinant in the quality of the interaction is the authenticity of the leader. Authenticity is about being real, being genuine. Genuine people know themselves; they are fully self-aware of their strengths and limitations and recognize they are part of the team. This awareness leads to a confidence that enables them to walk their talk, to deliver consistent messages, and to look people in the eye in a way that engenders loyalty. This is true charisma. True charisma embodies genuineness and authenticity.

So much has been written about the charismatic leader. It is bad enough that this publicity does a disservice to the other styles. Even worse is when people read about charismatic leaders and then remark to themselves, "that is not me," and in making that remark they break my First Law of Leadership. They make the choice to not lead. They are accepting the definition of charisma according to the popular press and the media and not the definition of those who are led. People in the ranks will tell you that charisma alone is shallow and is not charisma at all. Instead it is more about manipulation for personal ends. Passion is a better word to use here. Whereas charisma is often viewed as expansive and outgoing, passion can be quiet and focused. Charisma backed up with substance does inspire followers. Passion deeply inspires. In fact, passion can make someone charismatic.

This charismatic type of leader was elevated to icon status in the late 1990s in corporate America. The trait of charisma is often equated with good leadership, and there are plenty of examples of good leaders who were charismatic. But as Lt Col Ken Maney said, *"If all the leader has is magnetism (charisma) and inspiration then they will not go very far. People will see through it and know there is no substance."* There are many examples of people with charisma who could back it up with substance, but in and of itself charisma is not leadership. This is a critical point for many readers. Too many people look at those icon leaders of the 1990s and say, "I am not like that, that is not me, therefore I can't lead." And that is simply not true. It is not true when you look at the research on what makes an effective leader, and it is not true based on the comments from the people interviewed. It is far more important to know your own style and to use it to your advantage than to try to become charismatic and try to "pull off" something.

Jim Collins in *Built to Last*, and later in *Good to Great*, goes to great lengths to make the point that the charismatic leader may be more myth than truth. *A high-profile, charismatic style is absolutely not required to successfully shape a visionary company.* He does not say that visionary people are poor leaders, but he does say that great leaders need not be the iconic visionaries who so often seem to get all the media attention.

There is agreement that, no matter what style the leader employs, there must be an underlying focus and passion. Consider several quotes from the research for this book, *"Lt Col Jones was not charismatic but he had a presence, he trusted me, and I would have done anything for that man."* This passion and presence are some of the qualities that draw people near. *"Real charisma comes in the form of a compelling personality that is focused on the mission."* Another person said, *"If you don't care to the point of love, love of the mission and love of your people, you will not be a good leader."*

There are major misconceptions about military leadership in general, and Marine Corps leadership specifically. Unfortunately, the majority of America gets its understanding of the Marine Corps from Hollywood. It might surprise some people to know that physical abuse at boot camp is not part of the curriculum (*Full Metal*

Jacket), nor do Jack Nicholson-like war hawks go around talking about people not being able to handle the truth (*A Few Good Men*), nor are most junior officers inept simpletons (*Heartbreak Ridge*). The reality is far less flashy and even less newsworthy, unless you consider the legacy of success enjoyed by the Corps since 1775 as newsworthy.

The reality is that the Marines are a microcosm of society. All the personalities and social ills that exist in the general populace exist to some degree in the Marine Corps. Admittedly, the recruiting and indoctrination processes do a good job of removing some of the variability in the "people equation," but they do not erase the individual personalities and styles of people, including the leaders. Just as the Corps is comprised of people of all shapes and sizes, so, too, it is comprised of people of different leadership styles.

There are Marine leaders who are loud and forceful. Others are quiet and unassuming. They all accomplish the mission. They are able to accomplish the mission because, in their own way, they do the things leaders need to do to be effective. Beyond the leader are those being led. They, too, have unique styles and may respond more favorably to one style more than another, but they do respond. We may enjoy one environment more than another, but that does not mean we cease to perform in the one we don't like. In this case, the values and mission of the organization overshadow the leader. The true leader is only a part of the organization and works to further the mission of the organization.

There was full agreement from those interviewed that leadership is a developed skill. We are all born with a certain set of genetic traits. But from birth we must develop them. Our own personal preferences and aptitudes usually direct us one way or another, but we generally have the ability to make changes and learn new skills. Physical fitness is a good analogy here. All humans are normally born with the ability to walk and run. Some are truly gifted in this area and are "natural runners." Although some of those natural runners are sprinters and some are marathoners, running comes easily to them. Yet, not all athletes at the top levels are "naturals." Some work hard to compete at that level. And further down the ladder are the people who do not possess any superior ability to run fast or far. These people do run. They may do it at the local level or they may do it just for fitness, but they do it. Then further down are the people who do not run at all and are in poor health. Then one day they make the decision to get in shape and they start to run. It hurts; they persist and get better. They develop the skill of running. They are not world class but they are running.

Leadership is no different. Some people are born with the aptitude and desire to do it and they are naturals. Others are born with an average ability and must work at it. They study it, practice it, apply it, make mistakes, learn from them, move on from them, and get better. Like running, a program of development makes sense and can be very effective. Runners can develop a plan to get better by adding mileage and other activities to help them get better. Leaders can develop a program also. It will not be as regimented or structured as the runner, but the principle is the same. You will get better at it if you work at it. There are many examples of people who weren't born with world-class talent performing at a world-class level.

People require different styles of leadership at different times in their lives. People also develop different styles at different times in their lives
    Kelly Caulk
    Captain USMC
    Account executive
    International software firm

Civilian Example

I was working at an industrial laundry facility for a uniform company. We provided uniforms to companies and rotated them out and cleaned them. We ran two shifts. The manager I trained under was a screamer. He couldn't leave his office without reading somebody the riot act. Not only was he a screamer but he was condescending. I learned that his plant was about average as far as productivity and profitability in the company. In the three months that I was with him, I would guess turnover was 25 percent, which means it would have been 100 percent over the course of the year.

I moved to another facility for three more months of training. This plant manager was the total opposite of the first guy. He was soft spoken and not easily upset. His plant was in the top third of the company, and his turnover for the three months was about five percent. Of course, that meant his training costs were lower and his productivity was higher.

Both managers got the job done. They met their basic goals and each used a different style to do it. The soft-spoken manager had better results, and I am sure that is because of the way he treated people. Both styles worked but one worked a lot better.

Today you can't be a tyrant on the plant floor, or in the office, when people are working for near-minimum wage, or any wage for that matter. They really can get that wage anywhere. How do you react when one of them asks off work with a sick child? Do you treat the employee with respect, knowing you face similar challenges, or do you belittle him or her and threaten a loss of job?

It is amazing how employees can get back at you. I have seen it happen. I watched a salesman berate the mailroom guy for being incompetent, telling him how important it was for a certain shipment to get out immediately. The sales manager insisted the mail-room clerk address the shipment and put it at the loading dock for FedEx to pick up while he was standing there. After the salesman stormed off, self-satisfied, somehow his box made it to the bottom of the stack and didn't get in the mail.

Jeff Schade
Captain USMC
Consultant
National consulting firm

Marine Example

The first Group commander I had was about as intimidating a person as I have ever seen. He was of average build but he had a presence about him that was almost scary. He had an intense stare with eyes that saw right through you. He didn't talk much either. He observed a lot. When he did speak, his words were measured and evenly delivered. The productivity of the Group was great and it was a good place to work.

The next Group commander was a non-entity. He was as aloof as the first guy, but there was no gravitas to back it up. I don't think anybody ever got to know him because he was not around enough to get to know. He was always off doing something else and was rarely seen in the squadrons. The place became a miserable place to work. We lost our edge. You could see it in the readiness numbers, and you could feel it when you walked around. People were doing their jobs, but there was no sense of urgency. It was a rough eighteen months.

The third Group commander was different yet again. He was almost goofy, he was so lanky and so outgoing. But he wasn't silly. He was clear about the mission, and his passion for the mission was as deep as that of the first guy. He was verbal and vocal and always talking about something and always making you feel good to be a Marine and to be an American. He loved to laugh and he loved to have fun. But deep down you knew he would be there for you and be there right alongside you. Again, the productivity of the Group was great, and it was a good place to work.

The second guy was bad and it is a shame he got to where he did. The first and third guys were as different as you could imagine, but they got very similar results. Over the course of five years, it was a great lesson to me that we each have our own unique way of doing things, and that is OK. Today, as I look at new leaders, I see too many of them trying to be something they aren't rather than just being themselves. They need to develop their own style. I took parts of what each of those good Group commanders did, added it to my tool box, and made it my own. I also made sure that I wouldn't do the things the bad commanders did that made them so ineffective and alienated the men. One of the best things I did with that was give two close friends permission to "call me on it" if I was coming close to doing those bad things.

Mike Swisher
Major USMCR
Project manger
Database management company

SITUATIONAL AWARENESS

Self-awareness and comfort with style are valuable, but leaders lacking situational awareness are lacking a key component of leader effectiveness. Self-aware leaders can sense what is happening to them and the effect they are having on others. But they also operate in a larger context, and their effectiveness is often dictated by the conditions they are playing in. Situational awareness allows them to modulate their response to a situation.

The environment that leaders operate in is inherently variable. If this were not the case, we would not need leaders; everything could be put on autopilot. True excellence comes from great leadership AND a great system. Even the best leaders are challenged in the absence of a reliable system. Given a common process, much of the variability is reduced. Providing a reliable system or process is a function of management. Yet ten different people with different experiences and different styles, using the same process, will yield ten different answers, and maybe none of them is totally right. Such is the nature of something as non-scientific as leadership.

Beyond the processes, however, a great leader has a full range of traditional and emotional intelligence and the ability to consciously use different styles. Compare the great leader to the good leader who has less range. This latter person will get the job done but not to the level of the person with more range. And although we are all born with and develop certain styles early on, most people can learn to lead. People can learn to lead more effectively and more quickly when there is a plan in place to develop their abilities.

The ability of the leader to use different styles in differing situations is important. A leader may be more of the inspiring, pep-rally kind, but to be truly effective he needs to know when and how to use a different approach in a given situation. Leadership is not one-size-fits-all. This principle applies to the people we lead and to the situations we face. Different people may require different approaches. Similarly, different situations may require different approaches. And two different leaders may use two different approaches and still achieve the desired result.

Style can be described as the usual response or behavior a leader displays in decision-making and working with group members. Styles have been described as participative, autocratic, people-oriented, task-oriented, detail-oriented, and big-picture-oriented. Some styles are certainly better suited for certain situations, but generally, if not taken to an extreme, all styles can be highly effective. As pioneering leadership authority Ralph Stogdill wrote in the 1970s, "The most effective leaders appear to exhibit a degree of versatility and flexibility that enables them to adapt their behavior to the changing and contradictory demands made on them." As the demands of today increase and the pace of change quickens, this statement is more true now than in the 1970s.

Summary

One size does not fit all. There is no universal truth when it comes to leadership, and there is certainly no universal style that is most effective. Effectiveness stems first from the quality of the relationships between leaders and those they lead. The quality of the relationship has little to do with style and a lot to do with trust and credibility. Still, an awareness of individual style and the willingness to get better at adapting one's style to a given situation are differentiators of more successful leaders.

A fundamental ingredient in this is authenticity. Leaders should be themselves. Posturing and pretending are ineffective behaviors and they diminish trust.

Determining your natural leadership style isn't that hard if you are honest with yourself. The hard part is doing something about what you know about yourself. The true willingness to change for the better is one of the toughest parts of leadership.
Matt Green
Major USMC (deceased)

End of chapter application for
individual consideration and group discussion

1. What is your leadership style?

2. How did you develop this style?

3. Is it effective for you?

4. Is it effective in your current role?

5. What are your hot-buttons?

6. How would your people describe your style? Have you asked them?

7. Are you able to change your response based on the situation, or are you very consistent/predictable?

8. What changes to your style are necessary for you to take the next step in your career?

9. Do you coach people based on their style or yours?

10. Do you recognize when you are not effective?

Take Care of People

At Work
At Home
For Life

The relation between officers and men should in no sense be that of superior and inferior nor that of master and servant, but rather that of teacher and scholar. In fact, it should partake of the nature of the relation between father and son, to the extent that officers, especially commanding officers, are responsible for the physical, mental, and moral welfare, as well as the discipline and military training, of the young men under their command.
General John A. Lejeune
Marine Corps Manual, 1920

It helps when you know and use their name.
Trish Gibson
Lt Col USMCR
Federal law enforcement

At its core, leadership is about people. Fundamental to this concept is that leaders take care of their people. But this concept also uncovers one of the biggest clichés in American business: *people are our most important asset.* Countless organizations, and the leaders in those organizations, say this but the reality of their actions is far different. The message they often send is that the people don't really matter—it is all about the bottom line. The leader who sends the message that people don't really matter will generally not be as successful in the long run as the leader who is genuinely serious about taking care of his people.

Even today, perhaps more so today, in a society where individuality is lauded and autonomy is cherished, people want to know they will be taken care of. Part of this desire is instinct, stemming from our nature as tribal beings who need to associate. Part of it stems from the social contract that emerged in our society, and still persists somewhat, that says the firm will take care of us in return for a hard day's work and a full career. And part of it stems from the hierarchical nature of our institutions that says those at the top look out for those at the bottom; parents care for children, teachers educate and care for students, and employers take care of employees. Leaders then are viewed as having the responsibility for taking care of those they lead.

At Work

Beyond the expectation and responsibility that the leader will take care of the led, when a leader takes care of his people he sends a clear message: I care about you, I respect you, and I want you to be OK. In response, leaders gain increased loyalty from followers based on mutual respect. Ultimately this interaction results in better performance of the group. The thought process for the follower goes like this, "If I know you care about me, I will care about you and what you want done. However, if you don't care about me, then I will not care about you, and I certainly will not care about what you are trying to accomplish, nor will I work very hard to help you accomplish it."

A key question here is what does it mean to take care of someone at work? There are several dimensions and the interpretation depends on the individuals involved. This complexity underscores the intensely personal aspect of leadership that must be recognized to be truly successful. The best leaders get to know their people on a personal level and are able to tailor their approach to be most effective. One person may define being taken care of as being well fed while another may define it as having the right opportunity. Another may define it as recognition, and a fourth may define it as being well informed. How is the leader to know? If the leader listens to people and understands their unique needs and perspectives, individuals get the message that the leader cares.

Unfortunately, there are people who don't care about those below them in the organizational hierarchy, viewing them as inferior. Yet, the inherent value of a person has nothing to do with where he or she is in the hierarchy. The worth of people has nothing to do with rank. The real truth is that someone who occupies a position higher in the organizational chart is not "better" than anyone lower on the chart. Of course, one job description may exceed another in responsibility, but that does not change the fact that leaders are working with people who have value and worth.

I noticed that those who truly are concerned with every member of their organization, from the most important to the least, were the ones whom the men readily obeyed, even to the point of sacrificing their life as a result of one of your orders. Every member of an organization is valued, important to the cause. I think this readily extrapolates to the business sector and is sorely missing in most organizational climates. Though I am the senior ranking member of my battalion ("the CEO of Tanks"), I am no more valued than my newest Private, merely my responsibilities are different. I firmly believe that the intrinsic worth we ascribe to our members parlays into every aspect of the positive functioning of the unit.

Don Morse
Lt Col USMC

Some of the needs for being taken care of are relative. If I am cold and hungry then warm and fed is good enough, and I probably don't care as much about a pat on the back. But a pat on the back always goes a long way. Recognition is so easy to do. Thank-you notes, cubicle parties, and ice cream sundaes for someone who does a special job are all examples of recognition easily delivered. Make sure when you offer that praise that you are specific about the behavior you are recognizing. This way, everyone knows what to do and you avoid reinforcing the wrong behavior. An important point here is that some people in leadership positions view these small examples of recognition as a substitute for truly caring about their people. These are not gimmicks to get people to like you. In fact, an employee whose needs have not been met over time will view these attempts at recognition as feeble and condescending.

Another way to show respect for those you work with is to be punctual. Timeliness does matter. When the leader is late to meetings it says, "My time is more important than yours." When the leader is slow to respond to questions and to the needs that subordinates have to accomplish their job, it sends the message, "My time is more important than yours. I am better than you."

As humans, we naturally take care of people we respect. This mutual respect is essential to productive relationships. Caring is not the first word that comes to mind when we think of leadership, but that is one of the central themes from those interviewed.

If you don't care to the point of love, you will not truly succeed as a leader.
Pat Campbell
Lt Col USMC

Civilian Example

I encountered a situation involving two good people, male and female. He was in his early twenties and single, not a bad guy, not sure what he wanted to do with his life, decent work ethic, definitely an employee anybody would want, a solid "B" player. She was in her late twenties, single. Working full-time and going to school full-time also. A very good employee, an "A" player. Great with customers.

One day he left his wallet at home and he asked her for a few bucks for lunch. She agreed and said she would meet him in the break room with her wallet. As she handed the money to him in the break room in front of five other employees he said, "Thanks, but you don't have to pay me for last night, it was my pleasure." She ignored his comment at that time but later in the day told him she didn't appreciate the remark in front of her co-workers, especially since she was doing him a favor. He apologized and things got back to normal. Let me point out here that she has a thick skin and a great sense of humor, but it was the way he said it and when he said it that was the problem.

I talked with him that afternoon and plainly told him that his comments were inappropriate. I explained why they were inappropriate and tried to help him understand the importance of his behavior. I affirmed my support for him but also stated I expected him to confirm to the standards that every-one else did.

The next day he was working on his bike in the shop while he was on the clock. This is one of those things we just don't do here. When one of the employees mentioned it, he told them not to worry about it since we weren't that busy. But then he went on to tell the employees not to tell me. Of course, one of them did tell me and I let him go.

He wasn't a bad person but he was behaving badly and he was putting others in the shop in difficult situations, and I wouldn't have that.

Dave Lane
Captain USMC
Owner
Patuxent Adventure Center

Taking care of Marines and sailors is my highest priority.
Frank Simonds
Colonel USMC

Much of what Marines do is dirty, nasty, and uncomfortable. So any chance to provide some comforts, or to just show that you recognize the effort they are making, goes a long way. The corporate world also has its share of dirty, nasty, and uncomfortable jobs. It also has its share of clean jobs in which employees still want to know that the boss actually does care. For some leaders, this caring behavior or inclination to care is not natural. Perhaps their role models didn't do a good job in this area. Perhaps it is not their primary personality trait, but even these people can learn the importance of and methods for taking care of their people. What methods will work best? Get to know your people and find out. You could read a book like *1001 Ways to Motivate Employees* or you could get to know them and forget about the book.

So much of what we are talking about here involves respect issues. Leaders with high self-confidence and self-esteem have fewer problems with this theme. New leaders and those with less confidence are often more worried about themselves than their people, although it is the people who will ultimately determine their success. People will decide to go out of their way for you, or they will make sure that your important package always ends up at the bottom of the stack.

The end result of our people caring is that they will work longer and harder to finish a project and use their own initiative to do it without being told how to do it. For example, they will take it upon themselves to drive to Barstow (100 miles away) to get a part so we have what we need to carry out the mission.

Jim Chartier
Lt Col USMC

Taking care of your people often means going out of your way for them. The effort is well worth it. People remember it for years to come. Recently, a Captain was diagnosed with testicular cancer. His battalion commander remembers telling him, "Take care of yourself first and there will be work for you here when you are better." The Captain remembers it as, "You are a long-term asset to this battalion and to the Marine Corps; take care of yourself and the Marine Corps will have a place for you." Who knows the exact words that were actually used? But the truth, and the message the Captain received, was that he mattered and he had a home there. The Captain knew that the commander cared, and he responded with passion and an increased belief in the organization. Contrast this to the next example which does not end as positively.

Marine Example

I was part of a Marine Corps reserve infantry battalion conducting annual training at Camp Pendleton, CA. We were a couple thousand miles from home and had been in the field for two weeks. The Marines were tired, sweaty, dirty, and worn out. With our training completed, we had three days and two nights until we were scheduled to fly home. The Battalion had two options for lodging for those two nights. First option, we could find some trucks and get rides to a hotel-style barracks where each Marine would have a real bed, access to real showers, real food, and other amenities. Second option, we could live in a parking lot under a metal workshed which was in the same area where we finished our training exercise. We would have access to only a limited number of showers (public and cold). No other comforts were available in this remote section of the base.

The Battalion Commander asked the staff what they thought about the lodging options. Several of the staff opted to remain where we were since it would be "too much of a hassle" to find transportation, and once in the barracks we would have to clean them which "wasn't worth it for just two days." Some of the staff argued for the first option but were overruled.

When told they were going to be staying in place and not moving to more comfortable quarters, morale visibly sank. The pride of completing the exercise was erased. One of the Marines remarked, "I sleep on the ground for two weeks and now I get to sleep on concrete for two more days. This is my last trip." And, true to his word, he left the Marine Corps reserve when they returned home. Several other people made the same choice.

The leadership took the easy way out, to the detriment of the short term, the well-deserved, hard-earned, comfort of the men, and the long-term success of the Corps. The leadership violated an unwritten understanding: it is understood that hardships are often necessary—they come with the job, and people accept them. However, the leadership has the responsibility to take all reasonable measures to provide for the welfare of the "troops" whenever possible, and especially following periods of hardship. I was embarrassed to be part of that team at that point.

Tom Matkin
Major USMCR
Professional engineer

Do not lower your standards. Nowhere in here have I said it is acceptable to encourage poor performance. In fact, leaders who overlook poor performance are compromising their integrity. Unfortunately, many people I consult with view "taking care of people" as "coddling" them. They go on to ask, "Why should I coddle them if they are getting a paycheck?" Let's be clear, we should not coddle them. We should treat people as adults and expect the best from them. We should work to give them the best working environment we can, and we should implement timely and proper corrective action when necessary. We want to take care of them so they will want to take care of us. This extends to understanding what they are facing at work and at home.

AT HOME

Taking care of your people at home is more difficult to do, but that shouldn't stop you from doing what you can. In the military you often live in close proximity so you know when there are issues. There are certain expectations and conventions that the military has practiced for years. It is far easier to ask a nineteen-year-old Marine how things are going at home than it is to ask a nineteen-year-old civilian working for you in corporate America. The latter doesn't have to tell you anything, and there might even be some legal barriers.

No one is just going to tell you about things at home. You have to build up to that by establishing credibility with your people. In the civilian world we worry a lot less about personal and family issues by telling ourselves they are none of our business. Don't fall for that. They still matter. The crossover between personal and work lives is more pervasive than traditionally thought. Research shows that if someone is dealing with issues of any kind at home, there is a high probability that those issues will negatively impact on the job performance. The problem is, we often don't know our people well. Nor do we take the time and risk to know the personal situation of our people, so we assume and convince ourselves everything is OK.

It is far easier for leaders to maintain their distance. The last thing any boss wants is to become a listening post for marital problems or similar issues. We are not trained to have those conversations, nor do we want to have them since they are not about work. Sometimes those we lead will tell us things we really do not want to know. There are times when we politely listen and move on, and there are times when we must take some type of action to help the employee.

93

Make time for people: turn off the phone and the computer. Talk to them at lunch or on a break; bring in doughnuts. Remember their child's birthday, their anniversary. These actions begin to create a bond that pulls them to work. They want to come to work because they are engaged, and they also feel more comfortable talking to you about personal issues.

Kevin Baggott
Lt Col USMCR
Vice President
Fortune 100 financial services firm

Civilian Example

I was working in a union manufacturing facility. The job I was doing had me temporarily assigned there for several months, so I wasn't even in the chain of command. I was there as a technical advisor, but I had more tenure than most of the management staff except for the plant manager, so people looked to me for leadership when the plant manager was not there.

One week the plant manager was out sick. On Tuesday I saw one of the employees crying. I talked with her and learned her father was just diagnosed with cancer. The prognosis was that he had just a few days left to live. I listened: what else could I do? She wanted to go back to work. I asked her if she was sure and she said yes. A little while later, the union shop steward came to me and wondered if there was anything that could be done. Mind you, this guy was by the book, as was the plant manager. They both adhered to the union agreement very closely. It was not a positive relationship.

The woman had used all her personal time and wasn't entitled to anything, and, by the rules, no one had to give her anything. I asked the shop steward to get her, and I told her to go home and be with her father. She wanted to know how the days would be handled. I told her I didn't know but not to worry about it. The shop steward couldn't believe it. A few days later her dad did pass away. When she came back to work she was grateful beyond words. The fact that I helped her spend time with her dad in his final days was a debt she said she could not repay. I thanked her, made a comment about the importance of family, and we moved on.

The plant manager came back to work, and he wasn't exactly happy about my decision, but he couldn't really do anything about it either. For the rest of my time there, everyone treated me a lot nicer than they had in my first few weeks. I was no longer the guy from corporate. I was a caring manager who went out of his way, and bent the rules, to help someone. Whenever I needed anything after that, I always seemed to get it with no problems.

Vince Smith
Captain USMC
Quality assurance manager
Manufacturing company

This example is not that unusual but it is certainly not common enough. One of the reasons it is not common is that many managers are out of touch with their people and are not trusted or respected enough to be "let-in" on what their people have going on in their lives. Another reason they are out of touch is they view the employee not as someone who might need care but as a production asset to be used, discarded and replaced. Most organizations do a better job of scheduling preventive maintenance on their equipment than they do of taking care of their people. People want their leadership to know who they are and that they have value as a person. People want to be respected. By getting to know them personally and treating them as people, respect develops, tight bonds form, and great deeds are accomplished. This process takes time and effort.

Civilian Example

When I was a Battalion Commander in the Marines, I made it a point of making the rounds for one hour in the morning and one hour in the evening. I had a lot to do, and I had to make time to get out of the office, but it was worth it to get out and talk to my people.

Later, as a plant manager after I retired from the Marines, I did the same thing. There was always plenty of paperwork and meetings to get in the way, but I put it on my calendar and I did it. There were plenty of people in both situations who might never get to talk to me unless I went and talked to them on their turf. They might see me at an assembly or large meeting but they wouldn't get to know me, and I wouldn't get to know them, and we wouldn't have that personal connection.

When I visited the motor pool or the maintenance shop, I got down on the dolly and rolled underneath the jeep and asked questions and got to know them. I did the same thing at the plant. They knew I was interested in them. People are more comfortable in their own environment. In getting to know them, in reaching out to them, they began to trust me, and with that trust we began to build a team, and the team accomplished great things. Not me, the team did.

Stephen Oren
Colonel USMC retired
Business owner

Leaders of Marines, minimum wage workers, and white collar executives all express the importance of taking care of their people. They related the need to take clear steps to communicate their importance and your belief in this concept. Again, these are not tricks to get people to follow. Sincere recognition is what matters. And sometimes it is harder than others. Consider 75 Disneyland executives serving the nightshift breakfast at 3 AM. "It's a basic human need to feel appreciated," said Matt Ouimet, President of Disneyland Resorts. "It's easier with the dayshift, but the nightshift can be out of sight and out of mind if you are not careful."

This dayshift/nightshift culture or field/office distinction is dangerous and too easily created. It is easy to forget about the nightshift, or the guy in the field, when planning events. Over time, this behavior alienates employees, and alienated employees are disengaged. Disengaged employees are negative influences on the company because they are less productive. As in the Disney example, often the leader has to go to the employee. Also, creativity might be required to make sure everyone feels appreciated.

Marine Example

We had just gotten back from the war in Iraq. We were tired and ready for some downtime, but it didn't work out that way. We needed to support a major training exercise in Arizona. Normally we work two, 12-hour shifts but we moved to three, eight-hour shifts to ensure we had adequate coverage all day and night with the reduced staffing. That was fairly creative.

The Commanding Officer had also said that, when we got home, everyone would get leave whenever they wanted it. But then one section leader dictated a certain two-week period for everyone to take leave since that is the way it is always done. Basically, 50 percent of his section would be away each week.

Another section chief actually was scheduling leave for his Marines over the course of six weeks. He did so because he wanted to make sure he had people with the right qualifications on hand at all times so the unit could continue to conduct flight operations. His heart was in the right place because he wanted to support the flight schedule, but he was not acting in accordance with the directives of the CO. I told them both to let Marines take leave when they wanted to, as the CO said. It was that simple. I told them to let me have the conversation with the CO about not being able to operate because we didn't have the right people on hand. Then, if we needed to, we would work with our Marines to cover our obligations but not until then. Our primary responsibility was to get our people home to be with family and friends after spending months in a combat zone.

Eric Buer
Lt Col USMC

Out of sight, out of mind, does not apply here. Many jobs, military and civilian, require travel. It would be easy to think that, since the employee has no family to go home to while staying in a hotel, the family issues are less important. Actually, they may be more important due to the stress of separation.

Marine/Civilian Example

I was one of the Operations Officers of a reserve KC-130 squadron in upstate NY. The vast majority of the enlisted Marines in the squadron lived and worked in the local area. The pilots were mostly airline pilots who lived all over the United States and traveled to the unit to work at the Squadron on their off days from the airlines. Shortly after the attacks of 9/11, a 4-aircraft/100 Marine Detachment was activated in support of the Global War on Terror to conduct Marine Operations in Afghanistan and Africa. During the pre-mobilization planning process, we were informed by the Commanding General of 2d Marine Air Wing that he intended to move our Detachment of 100 Marines from New York to Cherry Point, NC and combine us with the Active Duty KC-130 squadron located there. Operationally, he believed this configuration was much more efficient than having two operational sites. However, it also meant we would be uprooting eighty-eight enlisted Marines from their families, as they would not be allowed to move their families from NY to NC for the two-year activation period. We knew that if we moved the Detachment to NC, we would be exposing our Marines and their families to a tremendous amount of separation stress that would hurt families and result in a number of problems. The most obvious problem was the potential traffic fatalities due to the 500-mile drive on I-95 that Marines would make as often as they could to go see their families because they could not afford to fly home.

Most Commanders would have just accepted the General's plan as briefed and told the Marines to pack up and deal with the outcome of the General's decision. However, we did not accept the plan; we knew we had a better solution. During very tense meetings, the Detachment Commander firmly presented our case and used every tool and resource we had available to convince the General not to uproot the enlisted Marines. Our Group Commander did a great job of being the intermediary. He allowed us to make a deal stipulating that we would support the Wing from NY and that the first time we missed a launch, we would pack the Detachment up and move to Cherry Point, NC.

This was a daunting challenge that seemed almost impossible to achieve, given weather in the Northeast and the maintenance-intensive nature of the aging KC-130. The Marines responded to the challenge. They knew the stakes and they knew we went to bat for them. Twenty-four months after mobilization, the Det was still in NY and we never missed a mission! Although this meant that some of the Officers had to spend more time away from their families to allow the enlisted Marines to spend more time with theirs, all the Officers banded together to make the plan work. It was the right thing for us as Leaders to do for our enlisted Marines.

Taylor Keeney
Lt Col USMCR
Airline pilot

Marine Example

In advance of the Iraq War, my Battalion was split over several bases in Spain, Italy, and Kuwait. The Thanksgiving holiday saw us half a world away from home with combat likely in the months ahead. Of course, even with the holiday we had people standing guard duty over our equipment in the various locations. I was in Italy and managed to get a flight to Spain to visit my detachment there. There weren't a lot of people but they were mine, and it was a holiday and they were going to know I knew they were there.

Shortly before my vehicle got to the first sentry, it started to rain. And I mean rain. Heavy, and it wasn't going to let up. I got out of the car and started walking the perimeter with my Marines. Rain gear didn't matter. We were soaked after a few minutes. But there we were, on Thanksgiving Day, walking together. As we walked, we talked about the unit, the mission, and home. I asked all of them if they had called home yet. One Marine said he would not be able to talk to his wife and kids because she would be driving to her parents when he got off duty. I told him I would cover for him on duty and to go call his family before they got in the car. I could see the appreciation on his face. I told others I expected them to make the call. If I just tell them to make the call, the words are hollow. But when I am out there in the rain and covering for them to enable them to go call, I demonstrate my commitment.

During my rounds I learned that one of the Marines liked to mountain bike. My son does, too, and I remembered that about him, and we would talk about it from time to time. When we got back from Iraq, I met his mom and she told me how comforting it was to her that we had kept the families so well informed and that we had taken care of her son. She then said, "And you too Colonel; you walked post in the rain on Thanksgiving; thank you so much." This Marine told his mother about my visit and she remembered it. Don't underestimate the importance of being visible and of truly caring. I was invited to his wedding, and I went.

Jim Chartier
Lt Col USMC

The cliché "don't tell me how much you care, show me how much you care," comes to mind with Jim's story. John C. "Doc"

Bahnsen in *Leadership: The Warriors Art* explains that *"caring consists of a genuine understanding for the needs and aspirations of others and a demonstrated willingness to act on their behalf. Mere words are not enough. Caring starts by looking them in the eye when you talk to them and listening when they talk to you. There is an art to listening that requires undivided attention and study. Very few people have mastered the art."*

Researcher Cynthia Fisher put it this way: "The percentage of time people feel positive emotions at work turns out to be one of the strongest predictors of satisfaction, and therefore, for instance, how likely employees are to quit." This principle of taking care of people is not simply about making people "feel good." It is about making people feel good so they want to work for you. Satisfied workers are more productive workers. Satisfied workers don't quit. The costs of low productivity and high turnover are real and have a profound impact on the success of any organization.

Marine Example

In March of 2004, Commander of Marine Forces Central, Lt Gen. Wallace Gregson, visited Marines at Camp Blue Diamond. He told them that what they were doing was important and they were making history. But General Gregson moved beyond the pep talk. He opened the floor to the Marines for them to ask questions and air any concerns they had. He was confronted with questions about "stop loss" and "stop move," the personnel policy that was making Marines remain with their units past the date they were supposed to move or get out of the service. He was asked about the UN and about the pace of the hand-over to Iraqi authority. This was a no-holds-barred talk. General Gregson closed his talk with a thank-you and "want you all to know that what you are doing here is very important. That's the most important message I want to pass on to you."

Lance Corporal Phillip Pitts, who was in the audience, was later quoted in a UPI story. "I learned a lot from General Gregson about what's happening on the political side...It is important that someone as high up in the chain of command as General Gregson comes and tells you that what you are doing is important. It makes me feel like there is a greater reason for being in Iraq."

Contrast this positive account with the much publicized, poorly delivered comments of Defense Secretary Donald Rumsfeld. When asked why National Guard units were not properly equipped to operate against the insurgents, he abruptly replied, "You go to war with the army you have." Unlike General Gregson, there was no dialogue, there was little explaining, and no matter what his real feelings on the matter, the message was, *I don't care about your problems.*

FOR LIFE

There aren't many organizations that will help you find a job once you decide to leave them. The Marines will. The official website at www.M4L.USMC.MIL describes the program, *"Marine For Life is a transition assistance program that helps Marines and their families get settled back in the community when they leave active duty. The program taps into the network of Marine veterans and Marine-friendly businesses, organizations, and individuals that are willing to lend a hand to a Marine who has served honorably. The Marine For Life program demonstrates that 'Once a Marine, Always a Marine' is not a slogan, but truly part of the Marine Corps ethos."*

Each year, approximately 27,000 Marines of all ranks are honorably discharged from the Corps. Twenty-two thousand of them are Sergeants and below. They are all imbued with the intangible skills employers beg for: loyalty, dedication, maturity, a can-do attitude, and an incredible work ethic. They are physically fit and drug free. Marine Reservists in the community act as "hometown links."

These reservists work in the corporate sector and understand the needs of employers.

Marine Example

Right now I have over 100 highly qualified Marines looking for jobs in the Raleigh-Durham area. My peers, the other hometown links, can say the same thing for their areas. These Marines have backgrounds in logistics, heavy equipment maintenance, information technology, law enforcement, and other specialties. They are drug free, know how to work hard, and follow orders. They make great employees. The Marine network is strong, and we want to tap into it and help our fellow Marines as they leave active service. Semper Fidelis (always faithful) is not just a catch slogan; it is a motto we live by. Marine for Life is another manifestation of us living it.

Bill Holmes
Major USMCR

At first glance one may dismiss Marine For Life as unique to the military. Don't miss the concept and the deeper message being sent. Transition assistance programs and graceful terminations are examples, in the civilian sector, of putting this concept of taking care of people and maintaining a relationship in place. People may ask, "Why bother? You are probably not going to hire them back." That is correct, you probably will not, but they are still out there in the marketplace with the opportunity to talk about your firm to peers and customers. What would you rather have, a former employee talking trash about you because of the way you dismissed him or talking well about you because you treated him with respect and dignity when you let him go?

This choice gets to how you truly feel about people and their development. It is of particular importance to those left in the organization. Those who stay can be saying to themselves, "Wow, I guess they were just using John while he was here. They really didn't treat him well. Maybe I should be looking for a new job before they do it to me." Or they could be saying to themselves, "Wow, they really valued John and the contributions he made. They treated him right even when they had to let him go. I am glad to work at a place where they truly value the employees."

When it comes time to hire people, the best pool is often those who used to work for you. A firm that laid people off with dignity in a downturn is well-positioned to get them back when the economy picks up. They are trained and know the rules and are ready to make a contribution. The return on investment in these people is higher.

Civilian Example

My father and brother had worked for the same company for a number of years. Both blue collar guys, they were never out sick and did high quality work. During high school over the holidays I would work with them also, sweeping, hauling, and other similar jobs.

In November one year a new general manager came in. His mission was to cut costs, and he didn't care much about anything else.

Shortly before Christmas of that year, while I was working too, we were all fired. My father had joined the Navy in 1941 at age 16. The war was over before he could even vote. He took pride in his work and in providing for his family which he always did, until the day he was fired. It devastated him. He had grown up in the depression and a job was to be treasured. Much of his identity was expressed in his work. I don't think he ever missed a day unless he was in the hospital.

To add insult to injury, the GM didn't even tell my father he was fired. He had the nineteen-year-old who was replacing him (at a lower hourly rate) break the news to him.

My brother was angry, I was confused; my father was wounded—literally. His health was immediately impacted. He suffered his first TIA (mini-stroke) a short time after that.

He got another job; we all did. But the impact of that experience on me has colored every termination I have ever done. When I have to fire someone, I know I am impacting their livelihood and the family of a human being. Real people are affected by my action, so I make sure I have no recourse. I coach, train, counsel, document and do everything else I possibly can so that if I have to let someone go, I know, and they know, I did all I could, and it doesn't come as a surprise. I treat people with dignity. Call it my Golden Rule of letting someone go, or call it Dad's rule.
Wally Adamchik
Major USMCR
Consultant

There are many reasons an employee may choose to leave an organization. Whatever the reason, it seems that once the employee decides to leave, many companies tell the person not to come back the next day. All of a sudden the employee is viewed as a disloyal legal liability. Rather than thank the employee for his or her service, security shows them the door. Sometimes there are intellectual property and security issues involved but not often. More likely, the boss thinks of the lost time and money invested in the person, the hassle of finding someone new one, and maybe even the "betrayal" of the departing employee after "all I did for you." Where is the dignity in that attitude?

There are some cases when the employee is forced to leave. Perhaps there is a change in corporate strategy or perhaps an injury prevents the performance of their original duties. These situations don't mean the person need be discarded by the company. The company has an opportunity to say thanks and keep the employee engaged. This action is not easy but it may be right. There is often a clear and compelling business case for doing the right thing. All too often, however, the right thing is difficult, it is not the easy way, and far too many managers opt for the easy way out. This choice is a failure of leadership.

Marine Example

General Mattis had a policy that all wounded Marines returning home from combat would have someone welcoming them home, updates to the parents on their medical condition within twenty-four hours, and a place for them to work if they wanted to stay on active duty. When someone in his Division was killed, no matter what service they were in, a Marine attended the funeral.

My Battalion has a sergeant who lost a leg and went home to Louisiana to recuperate. Once a month we sent someone from our unit to check on him while he was recovering. He decided to leave the Corps, but we kept checking on him. We flew him to Twenty-nine Palms to attend our Birthday Ball celebration. That was special for him because he knew he was still welcome, still one of us. He wasn't discharged and forgotten.
Jim Chartier
Lt Col USMC

While the opportunity for this type of ongoing care certainly presents itself more often to the military, it is not limited to the military. Organizations in the civilian sector can also show continuing care for employees after they have left.

Civilian Example

We had a senior account executive in software sales that was having trouble making quota. He had never had a problem before. At first we gave him the benefit of the doubt, thinking he would rebound, but he didn't. After three quarters, we had to address it.

He was having trouble adapting yet again to new advances in technology, and the relationships he had developed over time with clients were going away (either through people retiring or through changes in procurement processes). In short, he was burned out. It would have been so easy to show him the door since he wasn't making quota. But he was a good man who had done so much for the company in his nineteen years with the company.

We met with HR and crafted a sabbatical for him. Mind you, we didn't have a sabbatical process, but we developed one for him. After six months he opted to retire. He comes to visit from time to time, and I know he is coaching several of our sales people to higher levels of success—because he wants to. You know, if we had showed him the door he might still be talking to employees, but he wouldn't be saying nice things and he certainly wouldn't be helping them get better at selling.
Anonymous
National technology company

SUMMARY

Taking care of people is one of the fundamental responsibilities of leadership. It requires deliberate, intentional effort and sometimes the efforts of the leader will be rebuffed. That is not a reason to stop doing it. The return on investment of time and money in taking care of people is very high. Some of this return is quantifiable, as in the cost of lower turnover and higher production. Some of it is not quantifiable, as in the case of positive PR.

Taking care of people is about setting a standard and helping them achieve it. This approach is not coddling nor is it a sign of weakness from the leader. It is quite easy to dismiss people but it is far too difficult to replace them. It is far better to create an environment where they want to stay and they want to make a positive contribution.

It doesn't matter what they do for you, we have to treat them with human compassion.
Brooks Gruber
Captain USMC (deceased)

End of chapter application for
individual consideration and for group discussion

1. Do you think it is the job of the company to take care of its people?

2. Do you feel like your boss looks out for you?

3. Do you think your employees feel that you take care of them? How do you know?

4. What specific acts do you perform to take care of your people?

5. What impact do these actions have on people and productivity?

6. Have you ever been taken advantage of when you went out of your way to help someone? How did you react?

7. What one thing would you change about your work environment to make it more "people friendly"?

8. What one thing would your employees want to change to make the environment better?

9. Do you think that taking care of people is coddling and not part of what leaders are supposed to do at work?

10. What specific steps can you take to promote better care of your people? When will you start doing them?

Make New Leaders

Cultural
Personal
Accountable

All commanders should consider the professional development of their subordinates a principal responsibility of command. Commanders should foster a personal teacher-student relationship with their subordinates. Commanders should see the development of their subordinates as a direct reflection on themselves.
Warfighting

Mentoring and teaching. We, as officers, are charged with upholding that tenet in MCDP-1 (Warfighting). It still amazes me how many leaders (officers and SNCO's) don't have the first clue that <u>IT'S ABOUT THE PEOPLE</u>. . . . period."
Mike Finely
Lt Col USMC

How will your group function when you are no longer there? This is one of the classic questions for assessing the success of a leader. It is not good enough that you improved the department while it was under your guidance. What matters is that the group is able to sustain that high level of performance going forward. This recognition of the ongoing success of the company, or work group, is part of Adamchik's Third Law of Leadership: **It's about the organization.** Personal glory and individual success are noteworthy, but organizational achievement is the result of the work of many people over time. Nelson Mandela explained it this way: *"I am your servant. I don't come to you as a leader, as one above others. We are* *a great team. Leaders come and go, but the organization and the collective leadership that has looked after the fortunes and reversals of this organization will always be there."*

The age of the heroic leader is largely history. The iconic leader who stands above the rest is more fiction than fact. Organizations don't succeed by accident. Nor do they succeed because of one charismatic person at the top. Organizations succeed because of effective execution by those being led. They succeed because all members of the organization recognize the contribution they make to the greater good. These members contribute as a result of good leadership.

Growth and rapid change are synonymous with American business. It is the rare strategic plan that calls for shrinking the company or for maintaining the status quo. Ours is a growth world and growth demands change. Revenue growth is often the first bullet point on the strategic plan. However, all too often, the bullet points following that one fail to address the people issue. The company wants to increase sales by 20 percent over the next five years. A wonderful goal. However, who will oversee that increase? Existing workers will be facing volume they have never seen before. The traditional practice of "putting in some overtime" is no longer valid. Organizations should not rely on the ability to put in a surge effort to get the job done. The fact is that we are almost always in surge mode today. There will always be more to do than we have the time or resources to accomplish. The only possible way to execute at a high level is through a well-led workforce that exercises creativity and initiative. In the face of growth and change, tenured employees may yearn for the good ol' days. New workers may not know your system. Leadership is required at all levels.

The pace of change today and the amount of information people must cope with demand a more enlightened response. Leaders cannot get the job done by themselves. This fact forces organizations to become more decentralized in execution. A centralized system needs only that one competent boss. Decentralization requires proficient leaders in every level of the hierarchy.

CULTURAL

Leader development is cultural. Those leading the organization must *believe* that it has a worthwhile mission, that it will endure. A natural extension of this philosophy is that the people in the organization realize that developing the next generation of leaders is integral to future success. There must be an expectation of developing future leaders.

Author John Woodmansee said, *"The key to unleashing the potential of others in large part rests on creating the right climate in the organization. People who are uninspired by the nature of their work, lack confidence in their skills, are uncertain about their responsibilities, are concerned with being criticized for mistakes, and who rarely get feedback on performance, are unlikely to surprise you with high performance or innovation."*

Harvard professor John Kotter contends that "successful corporations don't wait for leaders to come along. They actively seek out people with leadership potential and expose them to career experiences designed to develop that potential."

Successful sports teams have good farm clubs. Successful businesses find ways to expose new leaders to lower-risk situations. The sad reality (and the reason so many organizations are unsuccessful or fail to thrive) is that most will not dedicate the resources—in time and money—nor do they have the expertise to develop leaders.

Civilian Example

We want to make fast, informed decisions. We also want people to grow in their abilities, so they will be able to support us as we grow. The only way this will happen is if we push decision-making down to the lowest level. We must give as much guidance as we can, and then expect people to run with it. We may make mistakes, but we'll recover from them quickly.

113

The biggest problem we have is the disconnect between saying we want things to happen at the lowest level possible and the managers who are either too afraid or too insecure to let that happen. This is demoralizing to up-and-coming future leaders, and we risk losing them when we do that.

Development of people, then, is a priority for our managers. This means our managers need to get better at delegation, coaching, counseling, and the like. It also means we need to identify people who may be future leaders for us and make sure we are providing them the opportunities to learn and be better prepared for the next level.

Keith Wolf
Captain USMC
Manager
National technology firm

The Marines recognize the importance of leader development and dedicate a significant amount of time to creating a climate that supports continuous learning:

Marine Example

In 2005, the Commandant established the MOS Roadmaps. An MOS is a military occupational specialty—infantry or radio repair, for example. MOS Roadmaps are intended to aid Marines in making intelligent decisions regarding their career paths. He encourages leaders at all levels to use the roadmap to mentor Marines. He adds, *"Marines are life-long learners. I encourage all Marines to continue their civilian education and to actively pursue the next level."* Of note, the roadmap contains recommendations for civilian education provided outside the Corps. This recognition that multiple educational perspectives yield more well-rounded leaders is important to note. The Marines recognize the need to challenge old assumptions with new ideas.

General T. S. Jones

Reading and discussion can be highly effective tools in leader development. The Marine Corps was the first service to establish a reading list for all ranks. When Marines think about reading, the "Commandant's Reading List" often comes to mind first. Recently renamed the Marine Corps Professional Reading Program, the intent of the program is based on the premise that "we must make time for reading... much as we do for physical training. It is not enough though, to simply read alone . . . we must read and discuss." The original objectives of the program remain:

A. To impart a sense of Marine values and traits

B. To increase knowledge of our profession

C. To improve analytical and reasoning skills

D. To increase capacity of using printed media as a means of learning and communication

E. To increase knowledge of our nation's institutions and the principles upon which our country and way of life were founded

F. To increase knowledge of the world's governments, culture, and geography

With very little modification, these objectives could be the foundation of a professional development program in any organization.

Marine Example

"How do leaders know if their Marines are reading? By talking to them, most importantly, by reading themselves, and by discussing their reading with their Marines." Colonel Carl D. Matter, commanding officer, Blount Island Command, aboard Naval Air Station at Jacksonville, selected Bob Woodward's book, *Plan of Attack,* for discussion. *"As Marines, it's important for us to read, and educate ourselves,"* Matter said. He wants his Marines to understand a bigger picture about the war in Iraq, and a somewhat dissenting picture at that.

"In evaluating a Marine as a warrior, we do not count the number of books read in a year," he said. "Instead, we gauge the capacity for sound military judgment. Yes, the Marine Corps certainly expects . . . in fact requires . . . the reading of books annually from the list. But the output we desire is daily display of military judgment that will serve our Marines and the American people in time of war."

As Commandant of the Marines, General Al Gray stated in the late 1980's, *"Success in battle depends on many things, some of which we will not fully control. However, the state of preparedness of our Marines (physical, intellectual, psychological, operational) is in our hands. The study of our profession through selected readings will assist each Marine's efforts to achieve operational competence and to better understand the nature of our calling as 'Leaders of Marines.'"* Extending General Gray's premise, success in business depends on many factors, some of which we cannot control. But we can be totally prepared for the challenges we can control and be as ready as possible for the unknown.

The concept of a professional reading list is not unique to the Marines. Many corporations sponsor a reading program. At the low end of the spectrum are firms that may suggest a book and then have a lunch and learn session at work. At the high end are organizations that give you the books and expect you to know them.

Civilian Example

We were acquired by another company. As managers, we would be doing the same job but the entire culture and the way we were expected to *do* the job changed dramatically. We all went to headquarters in Atlanta and had an intense orientation to help us understand the culture and values of the acquiring firm. Much of this session was conducted by the executive committee. Part of the orientation was an overview of the professional development path and the classes and reading that we were expected to complete. At the end of that day, they gave each of us a big shopping bag full of books from the reading list for leaders at our level. In fact, most trips to Atlanta for meetings would end with our returning home a bit heavier because of the books we were carrying.

Knowing that reading was an important part of the culture, I often made it part of the developmental objective for my people. It was not unusual during a performance evaluation to walk across the street to the Barnes and Noble to buy a book for one of my managers. We then agreed on a reading schedule and discussed the book over the next few months.

In fact, even today when I am coaching leaders, we might make a walk to the bookstore together.
Wally Adamchik
Major USMCR
Consultant

A professional reading program best includes periodical components (daily, weekly, monthly) and non-periodical components. The periodicals are the daily newspapers, weekly magazines (general interest, general business, and trade specific) and monthly magazines (general interest, general business, trade specific). The non-periodical would be books and other one-time publications, such as a white paper. The important point in all this variety is a diversity of perspectives to enable the leader to think more broadly and call on the experiences of others. This is learning at its best and it yields productivity at its highest. No matter what approach he or she takes, the leader is responsible for helping people understand what they are reading and to help them develop capacity to lead in the future.

PERSONAL

Development of subordinates may or may not be part of a given job description. However, whether it is written or not, make no mistake—the development of subordinates is a primary job responsibility of *all* positions. This emphasis on employee development is one of the key differentiators for the leader of the 21st century. "That's not in my job description" is an oft-repeated, albeit weak, excuse for failing to "grow" new leadership. Perhaps *coaching* and *mentoring* are better suited to describe the process. A leader may *coach* anyone at anytime, and will, hopefully, develop a *mentoring* relationship over time. (Mentoring means one-on-one, face-to-face interaction with the intent of preparing people to step into positions of increased responsibility and impact.)

Real leaders are always developing people. They recognize the interpersonal nature of the job and work to integrate individual desires with organizational needs. They create a culture that breeds learning and encourages risk-taking as a means to organizational longevity. Anyone can learn to be a great leader.

The good ol' Golden Rule is a fine place to start. How do you want to be treated? Would you like someone to look out for you and help you improve at what you do? Then, why not extend that courtesy to those who work for you? Maybe this was never done for you.

One reason may be there was no role model of proper behavior for developing people. Another reason might be an inappropriate sense of equity that says "no one really developed me. I learned it on my own; so can they."

Marine Example

General Krulak exuded leadership. He had integrity, he cared about us, and he was smart. He was always pushing us to be better. He was an avid reader on a wide range of subjects. He would ask what I was reading. Often, he had already read it, and we would talk about it. He would say, "If I have time to read and study, you have time to read and study." He was setting the example, but he was also making a point.

Professionals take responsibility for developing themselves first and then those they work with. All good leaders are lifelong learners and secure enough to know that they always will be. Good leaders know they can learn from everyone if they look for knowledge and are humble enough to be open to receive the learning.

Colleen Ryan
Captain USMC
Special education teacher

Job exchanges are often cited as an excellent way to develop someone. Employees spend a year in engineering, two years in marketing, two years in operations, and so on. Great concept, but only large corporations have the ability to implement it. (And ones where the leader recognizes the importance of building for the future.) However, you don't need a leadership university like General Electric to develop leaders. Much of leader development is informal, one-on-one coaching. Any situation can be used as a discussion point if the leader chooses to have the conversation. Every hour of the day presents opportunities to coach. The leader may take time to explain a decision, helping employees understand the big picture. The leader may ask an employee to explain the thought process involved in making a certain decision and then coach the person through seeing other courses of action. This behavior has value with all employees, but it is mandatory if there are to be leaders to step up to the next level.

Some employees are go-getters and are looking for the next challenge before they finish the current one. Leaders need to channel that energy and drive. These go-getters may not need a lot of training, but they still need coaching and the opportunity to learn new skills in handling new challenges. Your example as a role-model may be the most significant part of the development process for them. If your recruiting process is sound and your culture is supportive, you should have a number of these people.

Some employees assert that they don't want to move up. They say they are content with where they are and don't want the hassle of leading. They may not be truthful when they are saying this. Often they are really saying they don't have the training or they don't have confidence in themselves. It remains for the leader to create and sustain the belief that people can do something until they can sustain that belief themselves. This is part setting direction, part offering support, part providing education, and part providing opportunities to practice. Nurturing is a good word to use here. In situations like this, the leader goes beyond education and training but the ultimate objective is the same: To help people effectively step into leadership positions. Much of this interaction will be one-on-one.

Think of birds in a nest. At first, that is the only possible place for them to be. That changes. The mother needs to get them out of the nest. Leaders, too, need to help people get out of the nest.
John Brix
Major USMC
Airline pilot

Marine Example

I had a Staff Sergeant working for me who was ideally suited to advance to Warrant Officer. He didn't see it that way. He had defined himself as an enlisted Marine for over a decade. His frame of reference didn't include his being an officer. When I first talked to him about applying for the Warrant Officer program, he ruled it out. Over the course of the next year I made sure we talked about the idea on occasion, and I helped him see the impact he could have as a Warrant Officer and the opportunities it would give him.

When the application process started the next year, I again asked him if he wanted to apply and he declined, but I could also tell he was not as certain as he was the previous year. We talked about the opportunity and he did submit his application package. He was selected.

Now, years later, he has been promoted several times as a Warrant Officer, and he has thanked me for pushing him the way I did.

John Brix
Major USMC
Airline pilot

In the next example we see an equally profound impact being made on someone but the method used to achieve it is different. While the previous example shows leadership at the interpersonal level, the next addresses a larger scale. Yet, in both cases, developing leaders is the core message.

Marine Example

Colonel Zinni was an incredible teacher. I was 1stLt many layers below him in the chain of command. I saw him maybe four or five times when he taught Officer Professional Military Education (PME), but I no kidding knew what he wanted (commander's intent). We talked about scenarios, issuing orders, and how to handle situations as we advanced. The underlying message he sent was that he trusted us and that he needed us to help him accomplish the mission. He recognized it was his job to develop officers and he charged us with developing our people. He helped us understand that the main job of a leader is to make people better, and that is exactly what he did.

Pat Campbell
Lt Col USMC

Much of the development of leaders involves helping them learn how to think about the bigger picture. They are already proficient at the task, as we discussed in technical competence. That is why you are investing time in developing them. The piece they are lacking is how to operate in the gray area and how to influence people. We are actually helping them to learn how to think. The legendary 19th century strategist Karl Von Clausewitz in his treatise *On War* wrote, "theory is meant to educate the mind of the future commander or, more accurately, to guide him in his self-education; not to accompany him on the battlefield."

The goal is to have a bench full of people who can operate independently because they understand the issues. With the proper degree of independence, and with proper guidance in the form of commander's intent, they require less supervision and make timely decisions. In an era when time seems compressed and communication is electronically enabled, agility can be a competitive advantage.

Conversely, quick decisions can be a detriment to the bottom-line if the person is making bad decisions.

ACCOUNTABLE

Accountability is part of leader development. Accountability is not a bad thing. It is a logical extension of integrity and contributes to honest and productive exchanges. However, this ability to deliver feedback and have people receive it in a positive fashion stems from two distinct places. First, is the culture. As we discussed, does the culture support and reward leader development? Second is the leader. Does the leader have the interpersonal skills to regularly deliver effective feedback?

It is not my job to solve your problem. Part of being a successful leader is knowing when to say "this isn't my problem." Know who has the Monkey and draw boundaries. I can't solve your problem for you, and after coaching, if you can't solve your problem, maybe you cannot do the job for me anymore.
Trish Gibson
Lt Col USMCR
Federal law enforcement agent

People are often hesitant to make decisions, to think, and to act on their own, often because they have been stifled or the culture doesn't encourage such behavior. The truth is that a lot of our people do know the right thing to do. They are closer to the action and are smart. Subordinates use their leaders as safety nets. The challenge for a leader in developing new leaders is to respond with a question, rather than with the answer, when asked by subordinates what to do. Rather than offer your answer, offer the question, "What do you think?" They usually have it figured out already anyway. Or they certainly have an opinion. This process takes time but each time they are learning and gaining confidence. The role of the leader is to help people develop that confidence in themselves, to allow people to make mistakes, to share lessons learned, and to move on.

Civilian Example

Understanding the bigger picture and why we do things is very important. As Emergency Medical Technicians we are expected to make quick decisions. Literally, we are talking life and death situations. One of the problems we see with newer EMTs is the fact that they don't know why they do things; they just do them. They know they were trained so that if they see situation A, then they respond with solution A. If they see situation B, they respond with solution B. They reduce the decision process to the lowest common denominator and, in doing so, they miss the impact on the overall system.

For some, this is as far as they go, but the best seek out the knowledge required to understand why a patient is presenting in a certain way. What is the physiological reason for the signs and symptoms that I am seeing right now? It is at this level that they can make a more sound decision regarding the care of the patient. In fact, these are the folks to whom you entrust broader decisions. The good ones aren't just thinking about the care of the one patient that we are looking at right then; we are thinking about the others that may be involved, the care givers on the scene, the resources we have available, and the safety of everyone involved. To take it a step further, we are thinking about "what if" scenarios—"what if someone has a heart attack across town?"

Folks that can manage a variety of scenarios become the natural choice of the group to be leaders. Their decisions are sound because they are based on knowledge. The others look to them for guidance.

As described here, Situation A requires Solution A. Consider a situation involving the transport of a patient to hospital with ambulance and paramedics. What happens when we have two of these and only one ambulance and no paramedics? Who makes the decision about who goes and who stays? The simple answer is the leader. The more correct answer is the person who has learned or been taught the "why" and has assumed the leadership role at that moment in time.

Jeff Schade
Captain USMC
Consultant
National consulting firm

So much of developing leaders comes back to the ability of the leader to communicate. In commander's intent we talk about this from an organizational and mission perspective, but this is really about interpersonal communication. The art and science of communication should be mandatory study for a leader. Delivering praise, offering criticism, the timing of both are areas in which most managers need improvement.

In fact, the hard-driving type-A personality is almost notorious for delivering unvarnished head-on feedback, no matter what the human toll or emotional cost. They wrongly view this approach as some type of badge of honor and cite other methods as weak or touchy-feely. Going back to self-awareness, the goal for the leader is to modify the approach, or style, to be most effective with the person being coached. The ability to modify does not come naturally and requires practice. There are many fine books that will help you communicate better. I encourage you to work them into your professional reading program.

Civilian Example

My starting point is the understanding that it is my job to help you solve your problem, not to solve it for you. I had an employee who had come up through the ranks to project manager. She was really very good but she had started in project administration, essentially a clerical position, and she was always checking people, micromanaging really. This is what made her successful before and she continued to do it. The problem was she had become a bottleneck, and her people were doing less work, knowing she would pick up the slack for them.

She was not holding people accountable for getting their work done in the proper fashion and in a timely manner. I talked with her quarterly about my expectations for her and the changes I thought she needed to make. She resisted. The output of her group continued to be satisfactory, but she was running herself ragged and I knew the group could be doing better.

One day she came to me and said, "I have been wrong for the last three years. I need to supervise my team, not do their work." Somehow, the light had come on for her. From that point on she was more pleasant at work, since she wasn't overworked and the quality and quantity of the work her team produced was much better. This outcome took a while, but I knew what she was capable of and kept reinforcing and coaching and finally she made the leap.

Roger Brown
Captain USMC
Project manager
National technology company

The Marines are clear in their guidance to commanders that leaders at each level must be given the time and freedom to conduct proper training to enable learning and skill development.

Commanders are expected to develop subordinates and the out-comes should be viewed as direct reflections on themselves. This process is not always easy.

Marine Example

I was on leave in Hawaii with my family after Operation Iraqi Freedom. I had just spent nearly one-year in Iraq with my battalion and most of us were now home. We left elements of the battalion and would be rotating through.

So there I am in Hawaii watching CNN and I see one of my tanks in Fallujah that has been hit with RPGs (rocket propelled grenades). The reporter states that there were casualties. As soon as I hear that, I am ready to head to the airport and get back to California to learn what is really happening and to make sure everything goes right.

I called the battalion and talked to my executive officer, who gave me a complete briefing on the situation. He had everything under control and I asked if I needed to come back. He replied that my presence would not change things; the situation was going to take several days to evolve and there was no reason for me to come home. I still wanted to go home.

On the other side of this is my family. I had wounded Marines in my battalion and I knew they would understand if I went back to California. I had a very strong temptation to fly home. If I did do that my wife, and my XO, although they would under-stand, would both be unhappy. The best course of action for me was to stay in Hawaii. I recognized my desire to be at battalion, but I also understood my duty to let the XO handle the situation, while keeping me informed, and I knew that his development was one of my primary responsibilities. Flying to California would not have helped him develop. In fact, it would have sent the message that I didn't trust him.

Jim Chartier
Lt Col USMC

Leader development begins anew at every level. There is no way to be one-hundred percent prepared for the role you are about to enter. You can be well prepared but nothing will substitute for actually being there. This experience is true all the way up the chain of command. A new CEO remarked to me once, *"I thought I was ready for this. Not so. There are things that I simply could not be exposed to that I am now seeing. This is very different and I need to learn a lot."* This reaction occurs at most steps up the ladder. In fact, at the senior levels, where the stakes are highest, is where a lot of the denial of the need for more growth manifests itself. The "I have arrived" syndrome is prevalent at this level, and many new senior leaders don't think they need coaching or further development. This attitude is best dealt with before the promotion occurs. Again, this is part culture, but it is also the duty of the person to whom they will report to establish the expectation that growth, learning, and coaching will continue. Admittedly, this process may take on different forms as it continues.

Marine Example

A large measure of the effort in developing people is devoted to holding them accountable and helping them understand the context in which they must perform. I had a new Senior Drill Instructor. He had been a DI on Parris Island for two years and had done an excellent job. He was my number one DI. We promoted him to Senior Drill Instructor and he was simply not performing up to the standard. I sat with him and explained how he was not meeting expectations. It was not easy for him to hear that he was my worst of ten Seniors. We talked about it and he thought "he had arrived" when he was made senior, but the reality was he had new responsibilities and new challenges and he wasn't stepping up to them. He got on track quickly after that conversation.

Terry Williams
Captain USMC

Developing leaders is important for them and for the organization but, let's face it, it is hard work.

Many managers proclaim that people are our most important asset. They even admit to the necessity for developing leaders. When I ask them to show me, on their calendar, the name of the person they are going to spend time with today, or tomorrow, or the next day, in coaching and development, they are unable to do so. Managers schedule all sorts of things but why not the most important time of all, time to develop your subordinates. This may not be a formal meeting, by the way. It might just be that you make a note to yourself at the top of the day that sometime during the day you will spend fifteen minutes with Joe or Jane. If you are really serious about developing people, you will schedule time for this interaction and you will protect it jealously. If you don't proactively schedule the time for this important but not urgent activity, it will be displaced by more urgent matters, some important but many not important.

Civilian Example

I promoted a thirty-year-old employee into the lead estimating position. Although this employee was not the most technically qualified for the job, I selected him over several more-tenured employees. In his first few weeks on the job, he worked very hard at becoming a better estimator, reasoning that if he was the lead estimator, he should be the best estimator.

I took him to lunch and talked about the position and the future. I explained I didn't expect him to be a superior estimator. In fact, I didn't even want that. What I did want was for the employee to get a solid grasp of estimating principles and to be able to capably oversee the estimating function. The reason I didn't want him to become a superior estimator was that I fully expected the employee to move out of estimating in two to three years into a senior project management spot. I reviewed the roster of project managers with him and looked at the age and expected retirement date of each one. Several of the project managers would retire in the next five years. I explained I expected the employee to be around for a long time and that we would be running the company together for the next 20 years. The conversation ended with my saying, "Think about what I laid out for you, what will you do to fix your area. How will we manage this thing when the COO retires? Now that you know these things, what will you do?"

The employee then attended a peer group meeting with me. At this meeting he met with the Chief Estimators from six other firms of similar size and product mix. Talking with them, he understood more fully what I had been saying about the leadership role he would occupy in the future. Armed with this enhanced perspective, and with my guidance clear in his mind, we had a very animated and positive conversation on the flight home.

John Russell
Captain USMC
President
Russell Construction Services

Leaders must develop other leaders to enable the organization to endure and to succeed. It is a business imperative. That alone should be sufficient justification, but there are other rewards too.

The best leaders recognize that when their people succeed and advance it reflects well on them. Some supervisors are known for their ability to cultivate new leaders. Through a variety of methods they are able to produce a crop of new leaders for the company to use in new areas year after year. With their groups energized with people who are going to advance, the production of the group is normally higher.

Beyond the business imperative, perhaps one of the best reasons to develop leaders lies in helping others grow. It is incredibly rewarding to make a contribution to the maturation and success of the next generation of leadership.

Marine Example

I was the Marine Officer Instructor (MOI) at the University of Minnesota NROTC Unit. During the academic year I primarily taught military history to midshipmen and, with my staff, handled much of the military customs and ceremonies for the unit.

One summer I was tasked with being a platoon commander at Officer Candidate School (OCS) in Quantico, Virginia. OCS is where the Marines cull the herd. We don't want anyone to fail but we know many will. It is as physically and mentally draining as you might imagine. We want to know during that six or ten week period if the person has what it takes to be an Officer of Marines. We challenge them with near-impossible tasks and more work than they can possibly accomplish in twenty-four hours. Most will stumble along the way. We are interested in how they recover.

Throughout this period the candidates are closely observed. There is nothing they do that we don't do with them. As the summer approached, all I could think of was how physically demanding it was going to be. I remembered how hard it had been the first time, so the prospect of going through OCS again was not one I was warming up to.

I pushed myself hard. It was truly one of the most worthwhile things I had ever done. I had a tremendous sense of pride watching them graduate, knowing I did my part to help them accomplish this life-changing event. Knowing that I had made a contribution to the Corps.

Tom Matkin
Major USMCR
Professional engineer

SUMMARY

The best organizations consist of people who are ready to step up to the next challenge. They have a ready pool of able candidates who have been exposed to higher-level challenges, either through targeted opportunities in a concerted leader development process or through reading, study, and discussion. Within organizations there are leaders who are known and valued for their ability and desire to develop the next generation of leaders. Leadership development must be an integral element of the culture of the organization.

The standard is the standard; we never want to lower the standard. We do want to coach, mentor, encourage and help people reach the standard. Additionally, we want people to see the big picture, understand the context of their decisions, to understand the why, as well as the how. One of the major opportunities here is to help people see themselves at the next level. There are many reasons for someone's not wanting to advance. Most of these can be addressed because they are usually based on a misunderstanding of the opportunity or a lack of confidence in one's ability to perform in the new role.

Initiative, the willingness to act on one's own judgment, is a prerequisite for boldness. These traits carried to excess can lead to rashness, but we must realize that errors by junior leaders stemming from over boldness are a necessary part of learning. We should deal with such errors leniently.
Warfighting

Organizations exist for the long-haul. The work of leader development is not easy; in fact, there are many successful managers who have produced wonderful results while they were in charge. Once they left, however, the performance of the group decreased greatly. Why? They weren't leading the group and they weren't developing leaders for the next challenge. This is a leadership failure of the highest order. The best leaders make leader development a natural part of everything they do. They work at it and the rewards are worth it.

In the Marine Corps I never really thought that leadership is rocket science and I thought it wasn't sinking in, but something changed in me. Constant exposure to leadership eventually makes it second nature. The constant opportunity to practice and learn is invaluable. There is an accelerated learning curve as a Marine. I also know we can create the same opportunities on the outside.
Jon Hruska
Captain USMC
Group manager
National logistics company

End of chapter application for
individual consideration and for group discussion

1. Does the culture of your organization support ongoing leader development?

2. What percent of your time is dedicated to leader development?

3. How much time do you actually spend on leader development?

4. What should you be reading?

5. What should your people be reading?

6. Have you ever promoted someone who was not ready to be promoted? What impact did this have?

7. Define what a successful leader looks like in your organization.

8. Are your development efforts tailored to develop the skills defined in question seven?

9. Does your organization have enough people on the bench right now?

10. What are you doing to ready people for the next level?

Commander's Intent

Where Are We Going
Communication
Getting the Point Across

It all goes back to trust. I need to give ownership. I tell them what I want to accomplish and then let them figure it out. Leave room for them to be creative when you can, and they will surprise you with the results.
Jimmy Lane
Captain USMC

Imagination is that mysterious element that some people have a great deal of and others have very little of. People can be encouraged to develop imagination, however. Their leaders can tell them to explore beyond the immediate answer that comes to them when they are faced with a problem; they can tell them to reach out, not to feel bound by convention or anything else, to do the unusual or think of doing the unusual.
General Robert H. Barrow
Quoted in Karel Montor et al.,
Naval Leadership: Voices of Experience, 1987

WHERE ARE WE GOING

Where are we going, and WHY? This is the most basic question followers want answered. Yet it is the one least frequently answered today. Along these lines, much has been written about the importance of vision and the necessity for leaders to articulate one. Commander's intent differs from vision in that it is more specific; it deals with a finite objective, a way of behaving, or a desired result. More important though, both contain a future orientation and a picture of what the organization is moving towards. For example, a commander may have a vision of winning a battle. This vision then gets executed through plans set forth using commander's intent as guidance. A corporate CEO has a vision of being world-class in customer service to increase market share. The commander's intent for this CEO might specify training of people and systems enhancement as the means to this end.

In both cases, however, there is a future orientation. In both cases, there is something for subordinates to latch onto and use as a guide in their planning and in their daily behaviors. The importance of this concept cannot be overstated. "Commander's intent," was cited by *everyone* interviewed for this project as one of the essential elements of effective leadership. In the absence of this clear guidance from the leader, the group is uncertain in its direction and actions. Uncertainty leads to hesitation, which leads to marginal productivity and uncertain results.

Harvard professor John Kotter in his article, "What Leaders Really Do," offers that setting direction is the first priority of leadership. "Since the function of leadership is to produce change, setting direction of that change is fundamental to leadership. Setting direction is never the same as planning . . . The direction setting aspect of leadership does not produce plans; it creates vision and strategy. These describe a business, technology, or corporate culture in terms of what it should be over the long-term and articulate a feasible way of achieving the goal." He suggests that planning, a management function, is not a substitute for direction; rather, it becomes a complement to direction. The articulated direction orients the planners and enables them to focus their efforts. I spoke after a noted speaker at a convention once who stated that leadership and management are arch enemies. I totally disagreed then and I still do now. While they may be mutually exclusive in that they cannot be done at the same time by the same person, they are intimate allies and must work together.

There is a deep and universal emotion that underlies commander's intent. Trust. When a leader tells you what he wants to accomplish and lets you go do it, he is sending a message that he trusts you to do the job. This trust between people is the bedrock on which effective organizations are built. Roger Brown, Captain USMC, Project Manager, tells of being the scheduling Officer at a pilot training squadron that was not making quota. The commander came to him and essentially said, *"What we are doing isn't working, we are not making our numbers, I need you to come up with a plan to do it."* This clear direction and the implied confidence unleashed creativity in Roger, and he developed an innovative and creative solution to help the unit not only get back on schedule but get ahead of schedule. Roger's final comment is illustrative: *"He told me where he wanted to be, then we went outside the traditional method to use my plan to make it happen. I would have died trying to make that plan happen."*

The necessity of commander's intent in combat is self-evident. Everyone must know the intent of the action, the overall objective of the engagement they are involved in, and basically how it will be accomplished. Often in combat, leaders in the chain of command are unable to exercise command, either because of casualty, a communications failure (the radios aren't working) or the fog of war—that natural confusion resulting from the chaos of combat. In any of these situations, commander's intent makes sure that everyone in the unit knows the objective and is able to move towards it.

Marine Example

Operation Iraqi Freedom provides a recent and visible example of the implementation of commander's intent. Before the war, General Mattis, Commanding General 1st Marine Division, shared his plan with the entire Division and with all attachments from all services; every Marine, every person under his command knew what he wanted to accomplish, and why. Major Eric Buer deployed as part of Second Marine Division, but he has a copy of General Mattis's intent framed on his wall next to his personal citations. I asked why. *Wally, on the way over*

> *I was reading everything I could about the situation, the threat, the terrain, the battle plan, everything. As part of that preparation I read the commander's intent for First Marine Division and it made total sense to me. It helped me understand the big picture.* Another Marine, Major Ken Maney, USMC, who was attached to First Marine Division, concisely described the commander's intent in a way many Marines did: *First, do no harm, then be no better friend and no worse enemy. These words made it clear that there were many people in Iraq who were not the enemy, yet they reminded me of our mission also.*

Readers unfamiliar with the military might expect this practice to be sound and standard military doctrine, but this is not the case. Many armies have operated on a closely held command-and-control philosophy, eschewing the sharing of information. These armies did not want their soldiers to think; they wanted them to follow. The former Soviet Union was known for this, even to the point that many tanks in their huge tank armies did not have radios. They were to follow the leader. Of course, the limitations of this philosophy are obvious. By eliminating the leader, those units were rendered ineffective. Our society generally takes a different view of people and the contribution they can make. And this attitude manifests itself in the principle of commander's intent.

Doctrinally, commander's intent always includes purpose, method, and end-state. Commander's intent requires that each person in the organization knows the objective of the person two levels above. Thus, a squad leader would know the overall intent of the Company Commander. The Company Commander would know the overall intent of the Regimental Commander, and so on. These subordinate unit leaders do not know the intricate plans for that level, two echelons higher, but they do have a solid understanding of the objective and generally how the mission is to be accomplished. This awareness enables them to see how they fit into the big picture and operate accordingly. Otherwise they will be operating in a vacuum, separate from other parts of the group, and, as a result, they may act at cross-purposes to the rest of the group.

Let's move away from military jargon for a moment and put commander's intent in standard business terms we can all relate to and use. Vision, mission, and goals are all words that are in the same universe as commander's intent. The "V-word" gets tossed about by consultants and academics recklessly these days. They say a leader must establish the vision for the organization, or they must set the direction of the organization. And at the strategic level, that is absolutely true. However, we must look deeper than the strategic level. There is a tactical level to leadership, and commander's intent still applies. The intent may correspond to goals and objectives on a smaller scale, a local level, or a shorter time frame, but the essential point that remains is that all people in the organization know the objective(s) and the plan. Let's not get caught up in semantics. Different schools of thought and different consultants use the words vision, mission, goals, and objectives differently. Some say objectives are quantifiable while goals are bigger picture without measurable results. Others will say the exact opposite.

Again, let's move beyond the words and get to the concept. The fundamental point is that everyone in the organization knows his or her purpose, what the boss wants to accomplish, and generally how it will be achieved. In their basic doctrinal publication *Warfighting* the Marines put it this way: *the purpose of intent is to allow subordinates to exercise judgment and initiative.*

In business today this concept is often poorly implemented with corresponding results. The business unit, perhaps a company or division, is brought together for a big meeting (this may be a very unusual occurrence for the group, so people are already on guard). A senior executive stands up and points to a few bullet points on Power Point that are extracted from the recently formulated off-site strategic plan. He or she asks the audience if there are any questions.

Usually there are none. People are still shell shocked from having to be in the meeting, and they are still wrestling with what all that strategic stuff means to them. The meeting adjourns, and little is said about the vision and plan until next year. In the interim there was probably little focus, and even less discussion, about the vision. Intent, vision, mission, goals; all must be re-communicated and reinforced regularly so that everyone "gets it." When this process happens, a firm is energized and focused with predictable results on the bottom-line. Consider this example of this concept in action.

Civilian Example

I was consulting with an interior construction company in the Midwest. They install floors, walls, ceilings, and the like. Their Chairman told me he makes decisions on matters with customers as if they are twenty-year clients.

"Customer service is one of the ways we differentiate ourselves from the competition. Our craftsmen are great, and we are proud of the tenure they have with us, but I want to deliver more than a quality room. I want to deliver a quality experience for our customers, I want them to call us back and to refer us to their friends. They will do that only if they are totally satisfied with us.

The twenty-year perspective is a guiding principle for us. And it can be applied in two ways. The first one is from a historical perspective. Act as if this person has been a customer, a friend, for twenty years. Certainly, if they have been with us for that long, there is a level of trust and confidence built over time. Clearly, we perceive the relationship to be fair for us if we have worked with them for twenty years. With that in mind, we don't want to do something to ruin a twenty-year-old relationship. I tell my people to treat the customer like an old friend. When your buddy forgets to call you, you don't terminate the friendship. You get over it, and you move on.

From a looking-forward perspective, let's treat customers with the expectation that we are going to have a twenty-year relationship with them. This means that early on, we have to give them the benefit of the doubt. It is our responsibility to make sure we are communicating correctly and clearly. It is our responsibility to make sure we are delivering on the commitments we make. It is not the job of the customer to help us succeed. Yet, it is the customer who will decide whether or not we succeed. When we treat them as if we expect them to be a twenty-year client, we take the long view. With clients, we want them for a long time, so we don't fight over the little things and lose sight of the big things."

I work with this company often and I have had the opportunity over time to talk to clients and to employees. My conversations have confirmed what the Chairman was saying. Clients did feel that they received great service. More important, employees of the firm are able to tell me about this guiding principle, this commander's intent. Sometimes I will be introduced to a new employee on one of my visits, and I will ask him, "How do you treat customers here?" After the initial surprise, the response is always "treat them like they are a twenty-year client." When I ask them where this idea comes from, they tell me they know because the Chairman told them when they joined the firm, and they hear other employees use the phrase when making tough decisions with customers.

Wally Adamchik
Major USMCR
Consultant

Going back to the example of Major General Mattis, once he had issued his commander's intent in writing, he then took every opportunity to reinforce it when he talked with Marines in the weeks prior to the war. In fact, every Marine and sailor that was part of his Division during his time in command would hear from him personally before going "in country." He personally visited major units in the United States before they deployed to Iraq. Even individual personnel replacements coming to units in the field, as part of their orientation to the area, received a briefing from Major General Mattis on his intent for how things should be done.

I often hear people say that their people are fully capable of knowing and doing the task at hand, but the people do not know what to do next. Of course, they are not capable of knowing if they are not told. Commander's intent, or goal setting for a work group for the day, is a way of helping them know what to do next and to understand the context in which they do it. Understanding the bigger picture is important for employees in many situations.

Civilian Example

A new employee in an assembly line environment was working at a rate that exceeded the line standard. The line was rated to produce between 5.5 and 6.5 parts per hour, and he was working in excess of 7.0. While he was proud of his work, his pace was causing problems down the line where people were working at the target pace. His high output was causing a bottleneck at a workstation farther down the line.

When told to slow down, his initial reaction was negative. "Why don't you get them to speed up? I am doing my job well; don't make me slow down." The boss who doesn't understand commander's intent would have said, "Just slow down and don't worry about anyone else." This approach would contribute to poor morale in the employee, possibly lower quality, and an eventual loss of the employee to turnover. I acknowledged his frustration and then walked with him down the line to the bottleneck station. When we got there, it was obvious that station was behind because of his high output, but it was also very obvious to the new employee that the task being conducted at that workstation was far more complex than the one he was executing at his workstation.

We then talked about the workstation we were observing. We talked candidly about the employee frustrations. I went on to explain that the workstation he was on was an entry position and he was not expected to be on it for very long. Shortly, he would be cross-trained in other work stations. This system of training would give the line flexibility if people called in sick, and it would also allow job rotation to keep people from getting bored with any one task. The bottleneck workstation was the most critical part of the work done on the line, and I told him that I hoped he would be able to work that station eventually. Perhaps then we could find a way to increase the standard at that station and for the entire line.

Armed with information and an understanding of the big picture, he was able to return to his workstation and resume work at the standard rate.

Seth Hensel
Captain USMC
Production manager
National manufacturing company

This example illustrates how a manager took effective corrective action in a situation using commander's intent to help solve the problem. Let's look at a more proactive approach to communicating commander's intent. The Marine Corps personnel manual has a form called the Marine Reported On (MRO) worksheet.

This process gives the leader a consistent method for beginning a new relationship with a new subordinate. The form has space for a listing of the actual duties and job description the new person will be doing. There is also space for the leader to share his philosophy, values, hot buttons, and other items of importance. In most organizations these things often go unsaid, and the new employee is left to figure them out alone. The result usually entails lots of trial and error and some risk if subordinates cross a line they didn't know existed. This situation often occurs when someone with industry experience is hired by a firm. The person is hired because of his or her accomplishments, indicated on the resume. When starting at the new company, the employee gets an orientation from HR about pay and benefits but usually not a clear conversation about how, and why, things are done a certain way at the company. People assume since the new person has industry experience, he or she must "know" how to do the job. And basically that is true. But the new hire doesn't know the way the job is done at the new company. The person probably gets most of it right. But over time, there may be some quirks about style or protocol that become an issue. The performance of the employee is satisfactory but he just isn't fitting in. Of course, no one ever explained the ground rules for success in the new organization, nor did the boss take the time to lay out any expectations of the new employee. After that first question of "where are we going and why? The next ones people want answered are, "What do you want me to do? And how much of it do you want me to do? How do I win here?"

Marine Example

One of the keys to success as a leader is getting to know your people and letting them get to know you. They need to know I will go to bat for them. Every new Marine I get I sit down with and have a conversation about how I operate. Here is the score, here is how we keep score, here is what you can expect from me. I learn a lot about them from how they respond. It seems today they are skeptical about what we tell them. In the old days new people gave trust and respect, which the leader kept or lost through his actions. Today, it seems like more of the new folks want you to earn their trust and respect at the outset; then they will go the extra mile for you.

In my twenty-eight years in the Marines and after all the new bosses I had, I only received this type of in-depth, welcome-aboard meeting twice. Those two work groups performed at a higher level, and it was clear that the leaders of those groups were better at developing a high-performing team. What it did for me on the receiving end was give me some security and comfort about the situation I was entering. I knew where the boss was coming from. That conversation was the beginning of an open relationship in which feedback was welcome. In those situations we enjoyed a better flow of information, and the result was higher effectiveness.

I can't lead if I don't know what is going on. I need my people to tell me. If we don't have the relationship and expectations defined at the outset, uncertainty prevails. And people will keep things from you if they are uncertain about the outcome. That is not the way for a team to be the best.

Dave Lewis
MSgt USMC retired

The welcome-aboard orientation as scripted in the MRO worksheet, and as demonstrated by Dave Lewis, answers those questions the employees want answered. This jumpstarts the employees' careers at your firm.

COMMUNICATION

Clearly, conveying commander's intent is dependent on effective communication. The Marine publication, *Warfighting*, states that *a clear expression and understanding of intent is essential to unity of effort. The burden of understanding falls on senior and subordinate alike. The seniors must make their purposes perfectly clear in a way that does not inhibit initiative. Subordinates must have a clear understanding of what their commander expects.* Naturally, people want to know what communication methods work best. The answer is all of them. When it comes to issues of such critical importance, every available method should be employed. Communicate in writing, in memos and email, verbally in large meetings, small group meetings, and in formal (and informal) one-on-one meetings. Talk to people in their work spaces when you are visiting and walking around. On the flight line, in a fighting hole, around the water cooler, and on the plant floor you will find opportunities to reinforce what they are doing in support of your intent. And do not overlook opportunities to offer corrective action when someone is doing something counter to your intent. You undermine your credibility as a leader when you don't make corrections. Use all communication methods. No single method is going to get the point across.

Don't fall prey to the wonders of technology. E-mail and voice mail are great communication tools. There are some personalities that prefer to use them since they allow communication to take place without actually meeting with people. This method may be expedient and totally correct for certain communication, but there are other messages that need to be delivered in person. The accurate communication of intent is as important as its development. General Mattis made sure everyone heard it from him, verbally and in writing, and it was reinforced by subordinate commanders. But what about other situations?

Civilian Example

I was working with a construction company in a small Midwestern city. They had been in business for over 30 years, starting as a custom home builder and then evolving to high-end commercial construction and into general commercial construction. In early 2000, they conducted strategic planning and realized that they were in a risky situation. Their city supported them well but a downturn in the economy might mean less high-end work, and they didn't want that risk exposure. After careful conversation and research, they came up with two alternatives. One, they could take their operation to other cities and target similar construction opportunities. Two, continue to do what they always did in their home market but add production/mid-range houses to their portfolio.

Either option was a valid way to diversify and expand the business to mitigate risk in their home market. One other consideration for them during this planning process was that they had always prided themselves as family friendly. Therefore, the decision to move to new cities in the Midwest was passed over in favor of entering production housing in their home city. They wanted their employees to be home at night and this prefernce would not be possible with option one.

To their credit, they executed this plan very well. They conducted the big meeting and announced the initiative. It was well received by the employees. The firm went on to recruit the expertise needed to enter the production housing market correctly. Additionally, they conducted a strong marketing campaign. The initiative received a lot of visibility and reinforcement. All the while, they continued to operate in their traditional markets at the same level as previous years. There was no shifting of resources away from core competencies; they were building new ones.

Nine months into this initiative I consulted with this firm. I interviewed their chief architect who had been with them for seventeen years. He was responsible for the design of custom homes and high-end commercial projects. He was clearly well liked and well respected and his position with the firm was solid.

One of the first questions I asked was, "Tell me what this place will look like in three to five years?"

He matter-of-factly responded, "I don't know, I probably will not be here in 3–5 weeks."

I was truly dumbfounded and asked, "Why do you say that?"

"All I ever hear about these days is production housing. Clearly, we are getting out of the custom home business and I will be out of a job soon."

"Have you been told that?"

"No, but it is pretty obvious. We never talk about anything else."

After finding out that he had just updated his resume for the first time in seventeen years, I changed the subject and we moved on to finish the interview. I immediately went to the President and shared how his chief architect, the one who had designed some of the best looking homes in the city, was feeling. The President was baffled.

"Wally, I don't understand; we got everyone together nine months ago and explained our vision. We told them we were doing this to make sure we could handle a downturn. We told them this was protection for them. How could he come up with a different conclusion?"

"Have you repeated the vision since that day nine months ago? Have you reminded them that you are committed to custom work?"

"No."

"Sounds like it is time to recommit to the vision: A vision that includes custom homes and a reminder of the reasons you are doing it."
Wally Adamchik
Major USMCR
Consultant

GETTING THE POINT ACROSS

Intent is effective only if everyone understands it, so attempts have been made to measure how well it is communicated. In 2003, a multi-national study of a simulated Coalition Task Force was conducted to evaluate how effectively Commander's intent was communicated throughout the command team. This highly analytical report, *Objectively Measuring the Promulgation of Commander's Intent in a Coalition Effects Based Planning Experiment (MNE3)*, by Andrew Leggatt of BAE Systems yielded several valuable conclusions about communication of intent:

1) Despite access to and use of technology, Commander's intent was not well dispersed beyond the command team.

2) Level of understanding is affected by proximity to the commander.

3) Different levels of expertise in the participants cause different levels of understanding.

Looking at these few conclusions, the implications for business leaders are clear. Those involved in making the plan and those who interact regularly with the senior staff can be expected to know the plan better than others. Employees will have less understanding of the plan the greater the distance from headquarters. Familiarity with the plan can cause senior leaders, because of their proximity and involvement in the process, to take for granted that everyone else knows it as well as they do. This is a major error in communication of goals and plans and underscores the need for continued communication using several methods.

Employees with a higher level of expertise often require a higher level of understanding. This process takes time and it may cause a situation where there appears to be a clique of people who always seem to know more. This knowledge has something to do with ability but also something to do with seniors taking time to explain more to these people who are better able to grasp their plan in the first place. People see this better informed group and feel left out.

This study confirms what employees have known for years: Managers do a poor job communicating what is going on and why. The mandate here is clear. Communicate more, explain why, and use different methods. Don't forget the loudest communication of all, your behavior.

Without saying a word, you can send a message that totally undermines everything you are saying. An example of this is a situation where safety is an important component of a job. When the leader is not wearing all the appropriate personal protective equipment specified for a given situation, he sends the message to all who are watching that safety really is not important. The real message is "don't listen to all the speeches and all the training; the reality is we don't follow the safety procedures." Clearly, that is not the intended message but that is what comes across.

Another example of behavior's sending a poor message occurs when an experienced person takes a shortcut when completing a task. This person is able to do this and get the desired result because he or she knows in that situation it's possible to get away with it. However, the new employee watching this veteran on the job does not know what he can get away with. The risk here is that the job will not be done correctly or that the new employee might get injured. Setting the proper example is an important part of communicating commander's intent.

Your body language sends messages you may not want to send. If you are unsure about a certain course of action, there will be elements of your actions that say exactly that. Your voice may pitch slightly higher, you may avoid prolonged eye-contact, or you may angle your body away from the person you are talking to. These are examples that underscore the presence of a significant non-verbal component in all verbal communication. Even over the telephone, the listener can detect confidence or lack of interest. One solution for speaking with confidence on the phone is to speak standing up. Some fast-food restaurants place a mirror at the microphone the drive-thru order taker uses. This way, when talking to someone in the drive-thru, the employee looks in the mirror and is reminded to smile. These are two simple examples of increasing communications' effectiveness. Many of the leaders interviewed cited their personal study of communication as important to their success. This is a very important point we will see more of in our discussion of self-awareness.

Another way of characterizing how this communication interacts is that it must be congruent. All methods of communication must complement and reinforce each other. Any contradiction has the potential to undermine the entire message. Leaders must align their communications with their intent. This consistency generates trust and confidence in the leader. Alignment of communication is important but so is the alignment of organizational resources.

Commander's intent matters because it helps an organization employ a finite amount of resources. Alignment is the word many people use to describe this situation. An organization in alignment has all its resources functioning in direct support of the vision. These resources may be financial capital, people—individually and as a team—control systems, technology, research and development, equipment, and reward and compensation systems. Those are the major resources and your own situation may yield others.

The power of alignment is well illustrated by a comparison between a standard light bulb and a laser. Simplifying the physics, both devices emit light electrons. In the light bulb, electrons move in many different directions, and they are not directly working together. The laser, on the other hand, is a monochromatic beam of collimated electrons that move in the same direction at the same frequency and amplitude. The result is a highly concentrated beam that has tremendous energy. While a light bulb illuminates, a laser can cut like a knife. Imagine all your people moving and working with a similar focus of energy as if they were laser electrons.

On the negative side, imagine all your people acting as if they were coming from a light bulb and moving in different directions. Or think about your car being out of alignment. What happens? First of all, you have to work to keep it in the lane. This effort is tiring and distracts you from your primary duty of looking ahead and being safe. This situation also causes increased wear on the vehicle. Things wear out more quickly. There is increased friction. In an organization, this friction, caused by lack of alignment, causes people to tire also. The ultimate results are lower productivity, lower customer satisfaction, higher turnover, and other detriments to organizational effectiveness.

The alignment of systems is not always readily apparent and can be a tough concept to grasp. But when something isn't working well, misalignment is one of the first places to troubleshoot.

Civilian Example

I was checking into an extended stay hotel near LaGuardia Airport late one night. There were no towels when I got to my room, so I went back down to the front desk and asked for towels. The same clerk who had just checked me in said, "Sure, no problem, just bring me your old ones and I will give you new ones."

"Umm, I don't have old ones, there are no towels in my room."

"Oh. . . ."

"So, can I have some towels?" Mind you that right behind this woman was a stack of clean towels six feet high.

"I can only give you towels when you bring me your old ones." I pointed out the sign on the wall that said, you guessed it, "Customer Satisfaction is Our Highest Priority." The exchange took longer than I show here but you get the idea. Their system of towel allocation was not aligned with their stated desire to deliver high customer satisfaction. Not only was there a disconnect between the systems, but there was also a disconnect between the employee and the customer satisfaction statement.

Wally Adamchik
Major USMCR
Consultant

Another way of thinking about alignment is to picture a large black arrow on a piece of paper. Then consider what this would look like under a microscope or on a television screen. The arrow is made up thousands of pixels, tiny dots, that viewed in total are an arrow. Viewed separately, they are dots. When an organization is in alignment, all the pixels are in the body and head of the arrow, and there are no dots outside the lines.

SUMMARY

Those we lead want to know where we are going and why. By sharing this information with them, you send the message that you trust them. Trust is the bedrock of successful organizations, and it inspires the people we lead to go out of their way to make us look good.

Communication about your direction is critical and must be continual. You must vary your methods, but not your message, to reach everyone and to keep them aligned with your goals. The best leaders recognize the importance of communication and study ways to improve in the use of this skill.

Putting this all together is one of the biggest challenges a leader faces. There are market forces outside the company, competing priorities inside the company, and just too little time to spend on talking about issues. Yet in the talking we set the stage for success.

Just point me in the right direction and then get out of my way. I'll take care of the rest.
John Ruocco
Major USMC (deceased)

End of chapter application for
individual consideration and for group discussion

1. What is the commander's intent for you on how to conduct your job?

2. How well does your boss communicate his intent?

3. How well does your company follow that intent?

4. How well do you communicate your intent?

5. Describe the ideal of how your employees should act.

6. How do you communicate this to them?

7. How often do you communicate this to them?

8. What two things can you do differently to help your employees better understand your intent for them?

9. What difficulties are you facing as you think about this chapter?

10. If you don't do this well what are the risks for your group?

Culture and Values

Core Values
Alignment
The Science Behind Values

That two battalions of Marines be raised consisting of one colonel, two lieu-
tenant colonels, two majors and officers as usual in other regiments, that
they consist of an equal number of privates with other battalions; that par-
ticular care be taken that no person be appointed to office or enlisted into
said battalions, but such as are good seamen, or so acquainted with mar-
itime affairs as to be able to serve to advantage by sea.
(Resolution of the Continental Congress, 10 November 1775.)

I am a values-based financial advisor who will always strive to create the
best win-win atmosphere for you—my client—and myself. My team
understands that the client is the most important person in this office. We
never lose sight that terrific service, coupled with integrity and ethics, is the
foundation of your success. If any potential team members can't fully abide
by these concepts, then they can't be on the team.
Robert Watral CFP
Captain USMC
Vice President
National financial company

Born in 1775, the United States Marine Corps is rich in tradi-
tion and enjoys a deeply rooted culture. Core values are the fundamental glue that holds all of this together. For the Marine Corps, its
core values are honor, courage, and commitment. You will see the
following definitions on a visit to <u>www.marines.com</u>.

HONOR guides Marines to exemplify the ultimate in ethical and moral behavior as detailed in the following list:

- Obey the law

- Lead by example

- Respect yourself and others

- Maintain a high standard of integrity

- Support and defend the Constitution

- Uphold special trust and confidence

- Place faith and honor above all else

- Honor fellow Marines, the Corps, Country, and Family.

The qualities of maturity, dedication, trust, and dependability commit Marines to act responsibly, to be accountable for their actions, and to fulfill their obligations.

COURAGE is the mental, moral, and physical strength ingrained in Marines. Courage is the ability to do the right thing, in the right way, for the right reasons. It carries Marines through the challenges of combat and aids them in overcoming fear. It is the inner strength that enables a Marine to do what is right, to adhere to a higher standard of personal conduct, to lead by example, and to make tough decisions under stress and pressure.

COMMITMENT is the spirit of determination and dedication found in Marines. It leads to the highest order of discipline for individuals and units. It is the ingredient that enables 24-hour-a-day dedication to Corps and country. It inspires the unrelenting determination to achieve a standard of excellence in every endeavor.

All that looks good on paper but what are we really talking about?

Values have been described as an organizational, or personal, North Star— a constant fixture that guides us in the face of uncertainty. In the Northern Hemisphere, as long as one can see the North Star, he or she is able to navigate through any situation and arrive at the intended destination. Similarly, values enable people to confidently make decisions in the absence of any other guidance and know they are going to achieve their goals in a manner consistent with the expectations and behavioral norms of their organization. Values help an organization perform in the absence of the leader.

CORE VALUES

For one to succeed in the Marines, he or she must personally hold the values of the organization. Boot camp and Officer Candidate School are crafted to reinforce and instill these values in future Marines. Different people come to the Marines for different reasons, but once initial training is completed, they all share a common heritage and have undergone a transformation. They emerge from this initial training changed at the core, holding the values listed above. The Corps Values are the bedrock upon which all subsequent actions will be based. And all truly successful Marines embrace and model these values.

The culture of the United States in the early 21st century is one in which values don't get much attention. On the news and in print, we see daily examples of the degradation of fundamental norms. In this "all about me" society, people believe they are living in that old

Burger King commercial and can "have it their way"—all the time. To watch the media, it seems only people behaving badly receive praise and recognition. Poor behavior, ill manners, and even law-breaking seem to garner praise and recognition by our media. Consider music videos that are less about music and more about sex. Or Wall Street traders who are less concerned about shareholder value and more concerned about their own net worth. Church leaders, too, are in the news for adhering to a standard of self-preservation as opposed to the standard of a higher calling of justice and respect. In these examples, these "leaders" don't appear to have values worth emulating. In fact, their behavior perpetuates the "it's all about me" mentality, and these people are often rewarded for their misguided efforts.

Then, there is the single mother of three, working two jobs, just to put food on the table and a roof over her family's head. Or the recently downsized union worker who had his whole life plan turned upside down. These people are too focused on *survival* to be able to think about values, especially when they turn on the television and see rock stars flouting the same authorities the rest of us must obey, and prima donna athletes being paid millions of dollars for a few hours' work and juicing up on steroids to do it. "Why bother having values" people may wonder, "if they don't matter anymore?"

In the world of business, too, values receive short shrift. Business managers thrive on metrics and measurement. Theirs is a world of spreadsheets and cash flow projections. They wrongly perceive that time can be spent more profitably in ways other than discussing corporate values. When values are mentioned, perhaps in a strategic planning session, it is often in a quick and perfunctory conversation held to get the check mark for having talked about them at all. Then talk moves on to action planning. Managers cannot apply total quality management and six sigma to values. Values cannot be reengineered. They are not quantifiable, and, in the business world, "if you can't measure it, don't bother with it."

Values are tough to talk about. They are soft and "touchy feely," and no self-respecting business manager would want to go there.

Values are personal. People are uncomfortable talking about values, either because they are uncertain of their own, or because they have never seen such a talk held in the workplace. They don't know *how* to talk about values, or they are not encouraged to have the conversation. In larger organizations, people at lower levels have no interest in them. They see corporate values as something crafted somewhere on high—something they don't own a piece of.

When managers do talk about values, it is just that, talk. The employees know that the managers don't really believe what they are saying, or they may believe it, but the process and policies of the company run counter to the values. Compensation based on personal production, for example, will seriously challenge any values citing the importance of team performance.

Yet, Marines hold values that were crafted centuries ago. They live them and they talk about them. Values are not just on paper; they are the basis for all decisions Marines make. They may not be consciously thinking about values when they take action, but because of training and because the values have been deeply rooted in those individuals, they are able to take appropriate action. Different Marines might make different decisions in a given situation, but they will all act with the Corps values as the foundation for their decisions.

Civilian Example

My fundamental beliefs and core values are what matter. Everyone is different, so I have to be a role model for the way I want people to act in my company. Not only that, I must talk about these values and make them real for my employees. I want to encourage people to embrace these values and make them their own, at least while they are at work. But my values extend beyond work.

Family is important—it is most important. It is more important than anything we could ever do at work. I don't just tell my people that. They see me take time to go watch my son play hockey. We don't just have meetings at work; we have sessions in which we get to reconnect to our values. I start the Monday staff meeting asking about the weekend. I get specific and ask Joe how the fish were biting and things like that. We take some time chatting and I have had visitors suggest I was wasting time. But I want **whole people** to come to work; I don't just want employees.

A few months ago, we had an important presentation for a client for a pretty big job. Each of my department heads had a role to play in the brief. But then I heard that my CFO was going to cancel her vacation so she could participate in the brief. I went to her office and asked how things were going for the brief, and then, asked how her vacation plans were looking. She said she was canceling and I told her she wasn't. She told me the brief was too important; she told me she really wanted it to go well. I thanked her for her concern and restated my belief that family time is important. Had she known about the brief when she scheduled vacation, that might have been different. But she didn't, so vacation was the priority.

I then coached her through how she would delegate the task to her best person. We talked about giving clear direction to the person, helping her people prepare, rehearse, and her letting go, and going on vacation. Of course, the brief went fine. In fact, the client was impressed by the depth of our team and our willingness to let junior staff present for us. He was further impressed when I told him the reason my CFO wasn't there was that she was on vacation. His firm, too, placed high importance on family, and he could see the way our values were in alignment. We got the job. Was it because we are family friendly?

I don't know. I do know that if a tie-breaker was needed, that put us over the top.

The key thing to remember here is that we were guided by my values and the values of our firm. We don't win the battle every time we stick to our values, but, in the long run, we win the war.

John Russell
Captain USMC
President
Russell Construction Services

ALIGNMENT

Another power of values is in the recruiting process. The Marines have a reputation. People who want to join the Air Force, which is a fine organization, with fine leaders, don't join the Marines. The values of the Marine Corps attract a certain kind of person and yield a certain kind of result. People make the decision for the recruiter when they opt out of signing up to go to Parris Island (or San Diego). This choice of opting out lowers the cost of acquisition.

Every business needs people. The direct, and indirect, costs of recruiting, training, and retaining people are significant. Some research places the cost of hiring at two to five times base salary of the person being hired, depending on job position. Advertising, interviews, assessments, and drug tests all take time and cost money. If the values of your organization are clearly stated, people may decide early in the process that they do not want to work for you. A simple example of this is the declaration of a drug-free workplace. A candidate, knowing she will likely fail the drug test, decides not to apply for the job. Her decision saves you time and money.

The military, business, and the non-profit worlds are all alike here. When someone comes to your firm as a candidate for employment, the person is evaluating you as much as you are evaluating him or her. We look at the resume and ask questions to get a sense of what this person is really like and to see if they will "fit" the organization. Conversely, the candidate looks at us, the facility, and the people, and wonders if this organization is one he or she will fit into. Values are important here. If you embody values in your organization and work group, talk about them in the interview. Don't hand out a sheet of paper with your logo and your values printed on it and mandate your interviewees to read it. When you do that, you send the message that those values are not important. But, when you hand potential new employees that paper, and then *talk* about what those words mean *in practice*, the candidates get a clear picture. They either see themselves in that picture or they do not. If they don't see themselves in the picture, fine, they then decline a job offer or decline to take the next step in the interview process, again saving you a lot of time and money.

All firms face this challenge, but it is an even riskier proposition in the startup phase. Each new employee has a large impact on a small group. The 10th employee makes a bigger impact on the values structure than the 100th employee, who will make an impact but it will be diluted across 99 other people. Consider these two examples.

Civilian Example

We were hiring like crazy at the two technology firms where I worked. Demand was out of control and we needed to add people to increase capacity. It would have been easy to fill the gaps with people who were technically qualified to do the work. But we knew we were building a company to last, one for the future, one that could withstand a downturn. So the founders and the inner circle of leaders agreed that maintaining the culture was paramount.

We implemented a hiring process that jealously protected the culture. All candidates went through several peer interviews. In my interviews with them, I outlined our four cardinal rules. I also explained how we did not do things. I spent more time on this process if I knew the place they were coming from did not adhere to our values.

If a person passed all the individual interviews, we then conducted a final roundtable interview. This process was pretty intense. Some of it was scenario based. We wanted to understand how they would act. Many people failed here because they thought first about the technical solution rather than the core value that would underlie their actions.

I confess that this was time-consuming, but we never made a bad hire and, in the long run, that saved us a lot of money, and probably made us a lot more.

Art Glasgow
Captain USMC
Vice President
Technology company

This alignment process enables people to understand "how we do things around here." They may know the details of the job from their last place, but now they know the details of the way people do it at your firm.

Civilian Example

At 9G Enterprises we have a code of conduct, a set of principles and norms that define how we will treat each other, how we will work with clients, and how we will protect the brand, all the while delivering superior value to our clients. Many of our team members have military experience. Many, too, have been successful in business. You wouldn't think that these folks, former Generals, fighter pilots, even an astronaut, would need a code of honor to know how to work together. You are right, we don't need it, but we want it.

First of all it enables us to deliver feedback in the spirit of the code with no hidden agendas. In fact, one of the principles is to "make the call, accept the call" when something needs to be pointed out. Feedback is part of our culture. We look for opportunities to give it and get it. A few weeks ago, one of our facilitators received an above average rating on an evaluation and some specific feedback from the client. In most places this would have been tossed out because 30 other people rated this facilitator as superior. But one person had a different view. We told the facilitator about the comment, and, when he was with the client a few weeks later, he sought out the person who had made the comment and thanked him. He then had an opportunity in the session to talk about coaching and used that situation to point out how well it can all work out.

Second, our code keeps us very clearly focused on who we are and how we execute. Newcomers sometimes want to modify our approach to a way they had done it in the past. We explain they are more then welcome to do it their way; they just can't do it under the 9Gs flag when they do. We are not talking about robots. We are talking about a quality and integrity level that is superior. One person who wanted to work with us mentioned how he was looking forward to coming to our events and prospecting for clients for his business. We reminded him about The Code and how his behavior was inconsistent because it would be confusing to the client and there was a conflict of interest. He had a hard time understanding our point of view, so we decided we would not work with him. He is good at what he does, and he would have been a valuable addition to the team, but at what cost? The Code made it clear how to handle this situation.

Another thing about The Code is that we crafted it in the quiet times. While bullets are flying is not the time to figure out how we are going to work together. Now, in times of crisis, the norms are established, and we can execute in a superior manner.

At the outset I thought The Code was a little hokey, but I am a true believer now as I have seen its value.

Mark Turgeon
Captain USMC
Senior facilitator
9G Enterprises

The power of culture is as important for the mature firm as it is for the startup. It is not a self-sustaining process. Leaders become the stewards of the culture. Darden Restaurants is the parent company of Bahama Breeze (and Olive Garden and Red Lobster), an upscale Caribbean themed restaurant. They created the position of Minister of Culture for Bahama Breeze. This person focused on how people were getting the job done and made sure it was consistent with the overall objective of "providing a two-hour island vacation" to the guests. This was a senior leadership position. The leaders were committed to maintaining the culture in the restaurants and put their money behind that commitment. This action reinforced to all employees the importance of delivering that vacation experience. It is probably no coincidence that Bahama Breeze was recognized by *Nations Restaurant News* as one of five Hot Concepts for 1999.

Civilian Example

Although we are very large now, we are still a startup in many ways. New business units and initiatives are happening all the time. We hired someone from one of our competitors, and after a few days he remarked that at his old place it would have been empty at 5:30 PM but here people are still cranking at 6:30 PM because they want to. We don't have the stock option carrot like we used to in the mid-1990's. People are making money with the stock today but not like back then, so it must be something more that makes them work so hard.

It is our culture. We hire the right people, who are aggressive about the business. Everyone knows the business goals. They know what it means to them for us to grow. We communicate in memos, voicemail, video, one-on-ones, and every other way we can. This consistency of communication is essential to a good culture.

We recruit MBAs from the top schools but many don't make it here. They come in and think that because of their degree they "have arrived." Not here. Here they get a chance to work and prove themselves. They don't get a free pass to the executive suite. Our culture is not for many of them and that is fine.
Keith Wolf
Captain USMC
Manager
National technology firm

This emphasis on values and behavioral norms applies to the many non-profit organizations in our society as well. Some are interested in the environment, some in cancer research, others in social welfare. The point is that people choose to work with one of them, based on the beliefs and values of that organization.

In the absence of values, the workforce becomes too fragmented, and alignment becomes difficult. Alignment is manifested when all the resources of an organization are working in harmony toward a commonly recognized end-state or direction. The assumption is that everyone buys into the direction and dedicates a similar effort and approach to the cause. However, if my values differ from yours, my approach may differ significantly from yours. This different approach may be viewed as creative, when conducted within the norms. But this different approach may be viewed as aberrant, or maybe even criminal, if I operate outside the norms, as defined by your values.

When someone operates outside the values structure, it is the duty of the leaders of the organization to address the behavior. Yet all too often this crucial conversation is avoided. Perhaps the person is a high-performer who brings in a lot of money for the company. Perhaps the leader lacks the moral courage to confront the behavior. Whatever the reason, when a breach of values is observed, if it is not addressed, the values structure of the company is damaged and over the long-term can degrade with marked impact. The corporate accounting scandals of the early twenty-first century are examples of groups of people sacrificing their values structure.

Civilian Example

I was conducting leadership development for a billion-dollar privately held company. Half-way through the day, we got into a conversation about a customer situation that was somewhat dicey, and this conversation got very heated, very fast. Both sides were passionate in their arguments. Both sides were articulate in their explanation of why their solution was best. Both sides were inflexible. This went on for about twenty minutes. During this time, the CEO sat quietly at the head of the conference table. He pushed his chair away from the table, sending the message that he was not going to weigh-in on the debate.

Finally, the CEO leaned into the group and said, "Wally, do me a favor, put up your second slide."

My second Power Point slide had been a listing of their corporate values. I backed up a bit and displayed them on the screen. There was silence, and then the CEO asked, "Gentlemen, knowing what you do about this situation, and taking into consideration our corporate values you see in front of you, is there any doubt as to the proper decision to make?"

Again, the room was silent. Then, almost as one, they agreed on the correct course of action—the one based on their values. This course of action was more costly to the firm in the short run, but it was the right thing to do for their customer. And because of values, they were able to unanimously agree and move forward in perfect alignment.
Wally Adamchik
Major USMCR
Consultant

Another theme echoed by many I interviewed was the sense of being part of something bigger. A sense of doing something that mattered. This was again true in the Marines and in business. Gene Peterman, Sergeant USMC, Project Manager, national defense company: *The Marines are a big organization, but I always felt a sense that what I was doing mattered. I never felt lost. That started at boot camp, but it was reinforced along the way by the people I worked for. I try to help people I lead now to see that they are making a contribution to something. I want them to know that what they do matters, and I want them to know I will help them get the tools to make a bigger contribution.*

Ultimately, it is the responsibility of the leader to give people a reason for being there and to continue to be there.

Don't make the mistake of making value judgments of people here. I didn't say a doctor makes a larger contribution than a garbage collector. Our society needs both of these, medicine AND public sanitation. Both of these people can feel that they are making a major contribution. So don't confuse your evaluation of the task being completed with the sense of worth and value someone might have at doing the task. Know that as the leader you can contribute to that sense of value.

THE SCIENCE BEHIND VALUES

Anecdotal reports about the importance of values are interesting. And certainly the weight of these accounts is difficult to refute. However, there are numerous academic studies that support the concept as well. One of the distinctions between the military and business is the concept of rewards and commitment.

Micha Popper, in *Leadership in Military Combat Units and Business Organizations*, asserts that "in business organizations rewards are the major, and sometimes the only means of obtaining the subordinates cooperation, whereas cooperation in organizations like the military is also based on internalization of goals, and the subordinates are motivated by normative force." Popper goes on to refer to the different type of commitment, "distinguishing between instrumental commitment resulting from evaluation of the rewards perceived, and normative commitment rooted in the individual's personal values. The essential difference in the two lies in the psychological processes involved." Popper makes the point that, in business, people do what they do for the rewards. In the military, people do what they do because it is part of their belief system.

To accept this research at face value, though, is to deny the ability of leaders to "reach" people in a business setting without tangible rewards. We all know the reality can be different. We all know of situations where people remain in a job because they truly enjoy the culture and the environment created by the leader. This is true even when these people are offered the opportunity to move to a job with better pay. The other day at breakfast the conversation with an acquaintance of mine was about how much he hated his company. Downsizings and corporate scandals had made the place a miserable place to work. I asked how his resume was looking and how much longer was he going to stay. His reply says it all, "I am not looking for a job; I may hate my company but I love my boss and I am not going anywhere."

The psychological explanations of the emotional bond between the leader and the led are complex and worthy of further study for the true student of military leadership. However, suffice to say for our purposes the data show three basic ways of causing people to perform tasks: formal authority, use of reinforcements (positive and negative), and emotional influence. Of course, usage depends on the organization and the context in which the individuals are operating.

Research over the years confirms that pay is not the primary motivator. Issues such as proper recognition, fair treatment, and personal attention (when necessary) often rank higher than compensation as motivators. Dan Braun, Senior VP for Human Resources at the COLAS Group, a multinational highway construction and aggregates company, puts it this way: "People don't leave for the money, they leave because of these respect issues. When we respect people and create a culture that supports that behavior, we are going to be better off." Here, again, we see the importance of culture and values in practice.

Military units make it a point to talk about values and commitment. In effect, they are addressing the normative commitment when they do so. Business leaders talk about pay and rewards and are addressing the instrumental commitment when they do so. David Van Fleet, in *Military Leadership: An Organizational Behavior*

Perspective, presents the findings from a number of studies that investigated the differences, and similarities, of industry/business and military leadership.

He asserts that perhaps the Department of Defense said it best in comparing the four armed services in *The Armed Forces Officer* in 1965. *Each service has its separate character. It would therefore be gratuitous, and indeed, impossible, to attempt to outline a doctrine that would be of general application, stipulating methods, techniques, and so forth, that would apply to all Americans in combat, no matter in what element they are engaged.* Logically, this thought process transfers to business and our discussion of leadership as well. No single standard or practice will be universally effective. The military leader who transitions to business and tries to rely only on the normative will fail. The business leader who relies only on the instrumental is not capturing the true potential of his workers. However, the leader who joins the normative and instrumental is positioned for higher levels of success, as we have often seen.

SUMMARY

There are many fine examples of values at work in Corporate America, including Mary Kay, Ben and Jerry's, Timberland, and FedEx. There are many others that do not get the publicity but are equally noteworthy in their positive integration of values. And, with negative impact on the group, there are many leaders who don't realize the importance of embracing this crucial concept. They prefer to use the power of rewards—the instrumental approach. Yet, people are looking for meaning in their work and in their lives. In post 9/11 society we recognize that something deeper exists within all of us, and we want the opportunity to express it. As a leader, your articulation of values is an important step in providing that meaning. And in that meaning is the genesis of loyalty and productivity.

In 1996, Zell Miller, former Governor of Georgia, and a former Marine, wrote *Corps Values; Everything You Need to Know, I Learned in the Marines.* It is a candid handling of character issues that don't get much press these days: neatness, punctuality, brotherhood, persistence, pride, respect, shame, responsibility, achievement, courage, discipline, and loyalty. He agrees that the word "values" is a broad, generic term that has different meanings for different people, but he goes on to cite them as the *basic, bedrock traits that constitute the foundation upon which successful lives are built.*

Extending his premise, I would say that the values of your organization are the basic bedrock upon which success will be built. But these values have currency only if everyone knows what they are and *they live them.* The only possible way for people to know the values of your organization is for you to talk about them, model them, and integrate them into every action and decision you make.

Where is the Marine Corps? Is it at boot camp? Recruiting duty? On the front line? Perhaps, but, more important, the Marine Corps is our people. Wherever there are Marines who hold these values dear, then that is where the Marine Corps is.

Kevin Shea
Lt Col USMC (deceased)

End of chapter application for individual consideration and for group discussion

1. What are your personal values?

2. What are the values of your organization?

3. Are these in agreement?

4. Does your organization rely more on the instrumental approach of motivation?

5. How do you model the values of your organization?

6. How do you communicate the values of your organization?

7. When someone behaves counter to the values, how do you handle the situation?

8. Does everyone in the organization know what the values are?

9. Are values addressed by senior leadership in the hiring/orientation process?

10. What do you need to do as a result of reading this chapter?

Rehearsals and Critiques

The Foundation of Success
Practice the Way You Play
Let's Talk About It

Drills are a form of small unit training which stress proficiency by pro-gressive repetition of tasks. Drills are effective methods for developing stan-dardized techniques and procedures that must be performed repeatedly without variation to insure speed and coordination. Exercises are designed to train units and individuals in tactics under simulated combat conditions.
Warfighting

Don't be afraid to make mistakes. In fact, go ahead and make mistakes, that means you are trying. Most important, learn from your mistakes. Do this and you will succeed and people will follow you.
Owen Murray
Major USMCR
Consultant
National consulting firm

My father always said, "If you had time to do it right the second time, you had time to do it right the first time." Good leaders say, "To get it right the first time, you have to practice *before* the first time." And great leaders say, "That went well, let's take a look at what went right and wrong and see what we can do to make it bet-ter next time," as they conduct a rigorous and rankless debrief.

The concept of practice and rehearsal is one we often associate with performance activities, most notably sports and the arts. We don't think twice about the long hours a musician dedicates to practice. Nor do we question why a professional sports team practices throughout the year. Professionals, in whatever endeavor, practice to enable performance at a truly superior level. So, if they are that good at what they do, and have been doing it all their life, why do they need to practice? Especially late in the season when they know each other and are getting ready to go to the championships. Why watch the game films from last week? Deep down, we know the answer. We all know that regular and realistic practice, coupled with a solid critique, sets the stage for success at the highest levels.

THE FOUNDATION OF SUCCESS

Unfortunately, the concept of practice often conjures pictures from our youth of a taskmaster conducting monotonous drills at our expense and to our misery. Wind sprints, multiplication tables, and musical scales are generally not part of our fondest memories. So, as adults we do not have favorable thoughts when we think about practice. And yes, some of what we must practice as adults certainly isn't fun or glamorous.

Repetitive training on the very basic tactics is a pain, no doubt, but they are the building blocks of more complex tactics.
Vaughn Fox
Major USMC
Senior military analyst
Governmental consulting firm

Beyond the emotional baggage of practice, there are other reasons we don't place high value on these essential elements of successful performance. We often perceive ourselves as too busy to practice. The corporate environment often looks at rehearsing, or training, as a waste of time that could be better spent producing revenue. People may not take it seriously, because of poor execution, in which case it does become a waste of time. Or people don't do a thorough debrief so there is no learning, again, a waste of time. The most successful leaders and the most successful organizations make rehearsal and practice integral to the planning and operations process. No surprise, the success rate of these groups is usually higher than the groups that don't practice.

Practicing the basics can seem redundant. At some point, we think we know the task so well that we might not need to practice anymore. Yet, that behavior is a poor example for those still learning the process. Also, true expertise lies in the ability to apply the concepts and execute the basics while thinking about other things that are going on. For example, a quarterback doesn't "think" how he is going to throw the ball as he drops back to pass and reads the defense. That part of the task has become second nature, but only after years of practice.

Marine Example

Threat rings are lines we draw on a map to delineate how far an enemy threat system can shoot. For example, if an anti-aircraft gun has a range of 3500 meters, we would draw a circle on our map to depict that. In addition to drawing them on the map, in training we memorized the ranges of all the enemy weapons, and while we were flying our instructor would quiz us. We might be flying parallel to the beach and he would say, "OK, you get word that there is an SA-7 (surface to air missile) at the next bridge over the waterway. What are you going to do?" The first series of questions after that was always, "Where are you, where are they, what is the range of that weapon, are you in the threat ring?

These pop quizzes were a hassle; you never knew when instructors might hit you with one, and they could always find one to trip you up. Then somewhere along the way I began quizzing myself. Eventually it was second nature. I didn't think much about all this until we went to Iraq. Initially, all of the quizzing and questions was just a pointless exercise. In Iraq though, I realized that I wasn't "thinking" about threat rings; that part of my thought process was second nature. I was able to concentrate on the specific situation, the tactics, and the mission.

Looking back on it, I didn't know how valuable the training and rehearsing was. When I left the Marines and saw how little time was spent on rehearsal, I came to value it even more. There is no way people can become truly proficient at the task unless we coach them to do it and we work with them to make sure they know it well. If they fail to do it right, we need to first look at ourselves, as leaders, for what we didn't do right or what we might modify to be better understood. Only then can we look at them to see what they might have done wrong.

Bob Jablonski
Lt Col USMCR

Civilian Example

I was a sales manager for a small company and my team was invited to make a presentation to a very well-known Fortune 50 company. I had been working to establish this relationship for over a year. When the call came, I was hesitant, thinking we were not really in the running but had been asked to present to make it look like others had been asked. That happens sometimes when there is a favored bidder, but the company soliciting the work wants to make it look like they really were open to other bidders. The company called back to ask why we had not scheduled our presentation and I shared my concern. The company representative assured me we had an equal opportunity to get the work.

I got the team together and explained the situation. I facilitated a discussion on our strategy. We reached consensus on how to proceed, and everyone began planning their portion of the presentation. The team had five days to put the presentation together. I told them they would conduct several rehearsals along the way. They rolled their eyes when I said this. The presentation to the Fortune 50 firm would be on day six. We met on day three and everyone talked through their section while sitting around the conference table. Adjustments were made and the team went back to work. On day four we did our first rehearsal. For this, people actually stood and presented, using the actual visual aids they would use in the presentation. But they were just going through the motions and weren't taking it seriously. I explained the importance of the contract and why we were rehearsing. Comments and adjustments were made. The next morning would be a full dress-rehearsal. I instructed presenters to wear clothes similar to the ones they would wear at the presentation and to have everything ready as if they were doing the real thing. I also asked them to take it seriously, unlike the practice session they had just attempted. I then invited some executives from our company to act as the evaluators from the client. The team delivered the entire presentation. The executives asked them questions, some of which they could not answer. We conducted a full-debrief of the session over lunch, asking each participant what he or she could do better. I offered my thoughts and dismissed them to work on their sections and told them we would meet at the office the next morning so we could take the company van to the presentation and do final coordination.

We arrived one hour before the presentation and were able to see the room we were going to present in, enabling us to visualize and quickly plan our physical movements. When it came time to make the presentation, each of the team members was comfortable with the material and with the setting. This comfort contributed to a superior presentation. In fact, the representative said it was one of the best he had ever seen.

Of course, we were awarded the contract.
Steve Ripley
Captain USMC
Owner
Fawcett Boats

The concept of rehearsing a major sales presentation is not unique (yet too few firms make the time and effort to actually do it, despite knowing the positive impact it can have). However, the rehearsal concept has many other applications.

Civilian Example

Industrial rigging is the process in which pieces of mechanical equipment are moved into place in a manufacturing plant. These moves often involve large pieces of equipment, are dangerous, and no two moves are the same. Equipment may be one of a kind and the layout of each facility is totally unique. Throughout the entire rigging operation, speed matters. The firm waiting on the equipment to be installed is unable to produce anything during the down time. The firm installing the equipment might be paid a fixed-fee and will get the same amount of money whether the job takes two hours or two days.

I saw that our rigging evolutions always seemed to take longer than we estimated. Not surprisingly, the profit on the jobs was lower than expected, too. I went into the field and watched several installations by different crews. They usually did a good job of planning, but by the time they got to the job people had forgotten some of the plan. They were moving so quickly in different directions that the plan often went to pieces. I suggested they do a walk-through on site before the jobs. Predictably, this suggestion was met with skepticism and derision. It would take too long, it was a waste of time, and it wouldn't make a difference, were just some of the objections offered. I managed to convince a supervisor to give it a try, and I worked closely with that crew over the course of several installations to help them learn how to do a proper walk-through and debrief. The results were clear and indisputable. This crew consistently beat the estimate. An added benefit was that the crew was working more safely as well.

With the supervisor as an advocate for rehearsing, I gathered all the crews and explained the new procedure. Beyond this, we gave them training on how to conduct a proper rehearsal and debrief. We did group exercises that challenged them to build something they had never done before. A water tower from uncooked spaghetti and masking tape, for example, and more complex challenges. They learned how to plan better, how to talk about how the plan would be implemented in the field, and how to conduct a debrief once the rehearsal was complete and again once the job was complete. These newly trained teams went back to the field and the crews experienced success. The walk-through process quickly became standard operating procedure for the firm.

John Russell
Captain USMC
President
Russell Construction Services

Marine Example

As the Ordnance chief I am the senior enlisted Marine overseeing the ordnance handling and loading for the squadron. Peacetime isn't that hectic, really. Our planes rarely fly with full loads since it is so expensive. The Marines doing the loading get slow and weak. A 500-pound bomb really weighs 500 pounds. Yes, we have tools to help but there is a certain amount of muscle required to do any load. There are some types of munitions that we rarely see in peacetime, too expensive. But we are not a peacetime outfit. We need to be ready for high intensity, high tempo operations.

One of the ways I made sure my team was in shape was once a month we used inert ordnance and practiced loading and unloading heavy bombs for at least two hours non-stop. We also used simulators for some of the more sophisticated weapons so we would be familiar with them. The entire point was to have the Marines physically and mentally ready to go into overdrive. Sure, they grumbled when we were doing the drills, but they knew it was right. When things got busy in Kuwait, Kosovo, and Iraq, my Marines could keep up the pace. This would have been a lot harder if we hadn't been practicing all along.

Dave Lewis
MSgt USMC retired

Terrain models (mentioned in Technical competence) are scale models of an objective area. They are made with any available materials: dirt, string, cardboard, tape, and pieces of personal equipment. When time permits, they may be quite elaborate. In any case, they provide an accurate representation of the objective area the Marines will be operating in. Occasionally a model will be built to scale by experts in modeling. These terrain models are based on maps, pictures and other intelligence so the Marines are familiar with their area of operations prior to arrival. If possible, terrain similar to the operating area will be used to conduct dress-rehearsals. But in the absence of the opportunity to rehearse on similar terrain, the terrain model is appropriate.

Marine Example

Ideally, all units entering the objective area will conduct a portion of their briefing for their mission with all the people gathered around the terrain board. They will then walk through their actions in a larger area, perhaps the size of a football field. This procedure allows everyone to see how things relate, and they will go through the motions that they will use on the actual mission. Finally, they may conduct full-scale mock-attacks as the final part of the rehearsal stage. This is not training. Training was conducted in the days, weeks, and months prior. The details of this final rehearsal are as close as possible to the actual mission.

This type of rehearsal is not always possible, but successful units do what they can to allow time for such practice.

Our Marine Expeditionary Unit received the order to retrieve a downed pilot. We were going to find and recover Scott O'Grady, an Air Force pilot who had been shot down several days earlier.

We briefed the plan and then all the pilots rehearsed our mission in our ready room from start to finish, including all possible contingency plans. We then assembled on the hangar deck of the amphibious assault ship. While our aircraft were made ready for the mission, we walked through the mission again but this time with the remaining supporting units. We put masking tape on the deck to represent the geography we were flying into. We walked the mission from take-off to landing. Radio calls were spoken, and the men walked around the deck, in what must have seemed a comical manner to an uninformed observer, with pilots and co-pilots walking next to each other. Backup pilots observed the process and offered critique and commentary to enhance the debrief. The mission was executed successfully and was followed by a thorough debrief.

Ian Walsh
Captain USMC
Divisional Vice President
Fortune 100 company

Terrain boards, tape on a flight deck, or just talking through all phases of the mission are a standard part of the mission planning process for Marines. They attempt to make familiar something that was previously unfamiliar. This process reduces some of the uncertainty they might encounter on the mission. It increases the likelihood of successful completion of the mission.

Mission success in the corporate world is characterized by such things as improving on budget and schedule expectations and profitably increasing market share. Prototypes and rehearsals are examples of due diligence activities, before executing the plan, that often pay huge benefits.

PRACTICE THE WAY YOU PLAY

Rehearsals and practice must be done well. Poor practice is worse than no practice. Proper practice yields a well-trained group that is able to execute. However, due to certain limitations practice may not fully replicate actual conditions. Further, there are constraints that we may apply in practice that may have negative implications in application.

Marine Example

Early in the ground war in Operation Iraqi Freedom, my unit was to place reconnaissance forces on a militarily strategic hill. The weather was poor and visibility was marginal. The mission proceeded, and, as I (in an attack helicopter) approached the target, I fired one 2.75 inch rocket. Mind you I was carrying 38 rockets. I rolled off target and set up to re-engage the target. Again, I got the target in my sights and fired one rocket. I pulled off the target and realized the absurdity of firing one rocket each pass. Rockets are area-fire weapons. They are not designed to be used like a rifle, but more like a shotgun, which means multiple rockets should be shot at once. Further, I was in a combat situation and was needlessly exposing myself to enemy fire. On my next pass I fired the remaining 36 onto the target all at once. Several other pilots had a similar experience that night. Why?

In training squadrons we're not allocated enough ordnance to shoot thirty-eight rockets at once. In fact, thirty-eight rockets would be used to train several pilots on several missions with each receiving a few rockets. So, in training, we would approach a target, and, you guessed it, shoot one rocket. Then come around and shoot one more. This is a powerful example of fight the way you train, or play the way you practice. The peacetime constraint of limited ordnance is real, and I am not saying all ordnance training flights should involve firing 38 rockets at once. The principle is real, however. Rehearsals should be as realistic as possible. And where constraints exist, as in the rocket situation, that should be discussed as part of the training.

Anonymous

The scenario described above was not an isolated incident. In the air and on the ground, people defaulted to habits that had been well-established in training.

Marine Example

We were in blocking positions outside of Basra on the morning of day one. I was attached to a company of tanks, and the commanders had done a good job of briefing everyone on the rules of engagement. The gunners knew what to shoot at.

A gunner sees in his sights a Chevy Suburban coming at us across the bridge loaded with guys carrying machine guns pointed directly at us. The rules of engagement made it clear to the gunner that he was to engage, but he hesitated, as we all did. He asked, and received, permission to engage, and destroyed the vehicle. The next Suburban coming around the corner didn't make it as far.

We are so ingrained with safety and sanctity of life that it is tough to get past it. We preach it in our training, we debrief it after training, and it is tough to get over it. And while I am totally OK with that, I thought it an interesting illustration of the quality of our training and the duty of leaders to clarify very clearly the parameters of a situation.

Anonymous

Civilian Example

We were building a large upscale hotel for a major chain. Their architect added a number of new touches in his design. Some of these were cosmetic and involved the use of new textures and materials. Others were functional but not common to the hotel market. Of course, there is a lot of repetition in building a hotel. All of the rooms are similar.

Using this fact to our advantage, we actually built a full-scale mock-up of one of the hotel rooms in a modular building we set up for that single purpose. Everyone that had anything to do with building or installing something in that room was involved. From floors to ceiling and bathroom to closet, everything was exactly as it would be seen inside the hotel.

When we were finished we invited the architect and the owner of the property to inspect the mock-up. A number of discrepancies were pointed out in the inspection. Some involved quality of construction and others the owner's decision he didn't like something the architect had specified. We worked with the architect to make the changes and conducted another inspection. The final approval allowed us to perform more efficiently. First, it gave us the standard to live up to. When there were questions of quality, we could refer to the mock-up as the example. When new employees came on the job, they could look at the mock-up and see what the finished product was supposed to look like.

Ultimately, this process minimized the amount of rework we had to do at the end of the job.

The cost of the mock-up was shared by the major players and was easily paid many times over by the fact that the facility was opened early, and the waste of time and materials in rework was minimal.

Going through all that effort early in the project, before construction was 10 percent finished, takes a lot of dedication and coordination. But it also saves a lot of time and money in the long run and is very worthwhile.

Matt Rawlings
Captain USMC
Project manager
Regional construction company

The preceding example is about more than simply rehearsing; it is about developing the exact methods by which you will play the game. The principle of "you play the way you practice" applies further.

Practice is for everyone. Leaders lose credibility when they don't fully participate or when they merely go through the motions. This behavior sends three very negative messages to people. One, I am better than you and I don't have to do this. Two, this isn't really that important but you have to do it anyway. Three, when it comes to "game time" I may not be ready because I did not practice.

Marine Example

Each Marine infantry unit has a Marine Aviator assigned to it to help coordinate aviation assets. The belief behind this policy is that pilots understand what other pilots need and what procedures will result in better and safer use of the aviation assets.

This pilot is called a Forward Air Controller (FAC). Some pilots assigned as FAC's are not very happy about having to hike around and "play GI Joe" with the infantry for two years. They go through the motions except when it comes to the part about airplanes, but everything else is viewed with disdain. Often there are several FACs assigned to a Battalion. Consider this example about realistic practice.

There were two of us assigned as FAC's to an infantry unit. I got into it and played right along, doing all the things that I was supposed to do as part of an infantry unit. The other guy went through the motions. When we went to the field to do training, he would not dig a fighting position (known to many as a foxhole). He would not carry a weapon to the field because he didn't want to get it dirty and then have to clean it. He was an embarrassment to me because we were both aviators. The infantry Marines had some choice names for him. He showed contempt and disdain for them and they responded.

When we crossed the berm into Iraq, it was all live. And part of that meant that whenever we stopped for the night we would dig fighting positions. Imagine what it looks like now for this other FAC who never picked up a shovel in training. There is the occasional live bullet zinging around, he is getting blisters from digging, and none of the Marines are helping him. He was practically begging for help; it was pathetic. Of course, the reason they weren't helping him is that he had been such a prima donna in training.

It is really important to point out that, when we found out we might come under heavy fire, the infantry troops immediately pitched in, and he had his fighting hole with one of them.

Don't miss the point. As leaders we send messages with everything we do. And we need to be ready on game day because we practiced the right way all along.
Craig Blanford
Major USMCR

Let's Talk About It

People want feedback. They really do want to know how they are doing, good and bad. They might not like hearing the bad stuff but they want to know. Most of them really do want to get better. If they have no desire to improve, it may be due to a poor environment created by the leader. Ideally, this feedback is continual and not limited to an annual performance review. Continuous improvement is the norm today, and it requires ongoing analysis.

Marine Example

After Desert Storm I was involved with a group that was to backload Maritime Preposition Shipping. These are eleven ships fully loaded with the material to support a large Marine unit. The concept is to fly the Marines in and they join up with that equipment. This speeds up deployment since we don't have to fly the equipment in; it is already there on the ships. We were supposed to take eighteen months to reload the ships since everything needed to be restored to combat ready shape. The first ship took two months to load. At that rate, we are looking at twenty-two months. We did the total job in six months. How? Quality debriefs with team involvement to make each successive load go better.

Each team leader conducted a thorough debrief with his team and culled the key lessons learned.

Then these major participants would meet to review lessons learned and establish new protocols for the next load. Once we did that, we got the entire unit together and briefed them on what went right with the last one, what went wrong, and what we were going to do differently on the next one. Of course, much of what we were saying resulted from their input in the initial team debriefs. We repeated this process after each load. We completed the job in six months instead of eighteen or twenty-two. You can see the results of this continual implement and debrief-to-improve cycle.

On top of improving the process, we were involving the people who were actually doing the work. They know best the issues we are facing and when we ask them, it motivates them.

Jon Hruska
Captain USMC
Group manager
National logistics company

Critiques are an important part of training because critical self-analysis, even after success, is essential to improvement. Their purpose is to draw out the lessons of training. As a result, we should conduct critiques immediately after completing training, before memory of the events has faded.

Critiques should be held in an atmosphere of open and frank dialogue in which all hands are encouraged to contribute.

We learn as much from mistakes as from things done well, so we must be willing to admit mistakes and discuss them.

Of course, a subordinate's willingness to admit mistakes depends on the commander's willingness to tolerate them. Because we recognize that no two situations in war are the same, our critiques should focus not so much on the actions we took as on why we took those actions and why they brought the results they did.

Warfighting

Leaders set the tone in the debrief. This tone must be conducive to learning, with the leader often acting more as a facilitator, guiding the process. Occasionally the leader may be very directive in the debrief, saying something to the effect of, "You guys are terrible, you're an embarrassment," and then leaving. This has a place in business and in sports, but it is a card you cannot play often. This really isn't a debrief at all. The debrief we are talking about here is one in which people learn what went right, what went wrong, and how to make it better the next time.

SUMMARY

Practice the way you plan to play. Allocate the resources (time, money, people, and leadership) to do it correctly. Work with people to get better.

Debrief what went well and what you should continue to do, and share that information. Also debrief what went wrong and what should be changed, and share that information also. Critical analysis and review of the facts is essential, as is full and fair treatment for all players. When this procedure is regularly followed, people actually look forward to the accountability. They know the good and the bad will be addressed. They know no one will be called on the carpet or ridiculed. They know the sessions are for learning and development, and they come prepared to contribute for the good of all participants.

Most important, make this part of your culture. Develop the habit of delivering feedback to your team. Ask for their input also. They have brains and take pride in what they do, and they want to get better at it; just ask them.

Don't even attempt to do the things outlined in this chapter unless you are willing to make the commitment to execute them well. To do differently sends the signal that you really don't care. If you don't care, I guarantee that your subordinates will not care. You cannot accomplish great things with a disinterested workforce. You can achieve greatness with one that believes in continuous improvement that starts at the top.

The only way you can possibly get better at what you do is to talk about how you are doing. Too often we avoid these conversations since we don't want to hurt feelings. You will never get better that way.
Clark Cox
Captain USMC (deceased)

End of chapter application for individual consideration and for group discussion

1. What is your opinion of practice? Training? Rehearsing?

2. Is there opportunity to apply this concept in your business?

3. What is the company attitude toward taking time for rehearsal and practice?

4. How do you measure the return on investment of this time?

5. Describe a situation that, looking back on it, some type of rehearsal would have been beneficial. What about the outcome of the situation might have changed?

6. What issues at your business are repeat issues?

7. What is the cost of these ongoing defects and challenges?

8. What will you do to eliminate them?

9. What steps are you taking to get better?

10. How well do you conduct after action discussions? What can you do to improve this process?

About the Author

In his youth, Wally often worked with his father and brother in construction. Both master craftsmen, they insisted upon top-quality work. He learned more about excellence from his mother, who was the first woman to referee a basketball game at Madison Square Garden. His parents encouraged him to achieve and he now encourages others to do the same.

At the University of Notre Dame, Wally was the mascot—the Leprechaun. Rain or shine. Home or away, Wally put 100 percent of himself into the game. This same level of commitment defines his work today. His total focus is on meeting your needs and delivering tailored solutions to make a positive and lasting effect on your business.

As an Officer of Marines, Wally deployed throughout the world. He is qualified in several specialties, including armor and as a pilot of AH-1W Super Cobra attack helicopters. His years in the Corps honed his motivational and leadership skills. His influence remains in a legacy of Marines who provide inspired leadership for this country and for their organizations.

Seeking a new challenge, Wally entered the private sector. He was recognized for superior performance and award-winning leadership at two national restaurant companies. At the same time he earned his MBA from the University of North Carolina at Chapel Hill.

He then moved into consulting and speaking. His solutions are practical, profitable, and powerful. He understands the Fortune 500 firm as well as he does the family business and is able to modify his approach to make an impact in both.

Practicing what he preaches about family balance and quality of life, Wally schedules time with his wife and two children. They live in Raleigh, NC.

Please contact Wally about speaking and consulting, at:
Wally Adamchik
FireStarter Speaking and Consulting
919-673-9499
wally@ beafirestarter.com
www.beafirestarter.com